Dream Catcher 51

Stairwell Books

Dream Catcher 51

**Editor Emeritus
And Founder**
Paul Sutherland

Editor
Hannah Stone

Editorial Board
John Gilham (Retired Editor)
Amina Alyal (Retired Editor)
Tanya Parker Nightingale
Pauline Kirk
Rose Drew
Alan Gillott
Joe Williams
Mia Lofthouse
Will Kemp
Laura Strickland
Greg McGee

Art Advisor
Greg McGee

Production Managers
Alan Gillott and Rose Drew

Subscriptions to
Dream Catcher
Magazine

£18.00 UK (Two issues inc. p&p)
£25.00 Europe
£28.00 USA and Canada

Cheques should be made
payable to **Dream Catcher**
and sent to:

Dream Catcher Subscriptions
161 Lowther Street
York, YO31 7LZ
UK

+44 1904 733767

argillott@gmail.com

www.dreamcatchermagazine.co.uk
@literaryartsmag
www.stairwellbooks.co.uk
@stairwellbooks

Dream Catcher Magazine

Dream Catcher No. 51

© Adam Strickson, Andrew Pearson, Andrew Senior, Andria Jane Cooke, Angela Brodie, Ann Preston, Annie Kocur, Barbara Howerska, Carolyn Oulton, Cathryn M. Spiller, Charles Lomas, Christopher Webster, Claire Booker, Clare Bryden, Clare Starling, Clifford Liles, Connie Greig, Cosmo Goldsmith, Craig Martin Getz, D G Herring, Dave Foxton, Dave Wynne-Jones, David Olsen, David Sapp, Denise Bennett, Elaine Ewart, Greg Forshaw, Greg McGee, Hannah Stone, Heather Deckner, Helen Scadding, Ian Chapman, Jack Granath, Jane Newberry, Jean Atkin, Jennifer Harrison, Jet McDonald, John Scarborough, Kat Couch, Keith Willson, Kristina Diprose, Laura Reanna Smith, Lauren K. Nixon, Lisa Falshaw, Louise Worthington, Marius Grose, Mark Pearce, Martin Reed, Nick Allen, Nick Cooke, Pamela Coren, Patrick Lodge, Paul Bavister, Paul Brownsey, Pauline Kirk, Phil Knight, Phil Vernon, Rachel Goodman, Ralph Dartford, Ray Malone, Richard Smith, Rosie Jackson, Sarah J Bryson, Shaun Barr, Simon French, Simon Tindale, Stuart Handysides, Sue Spiers, Tom Ratcliffe, Tom Vaughan, Wilf Deckner,
2025

The moral rights of authors and artists have been asserted
No part of this book may be used or reproduced in any manner for the purpose of training artificial intelligence technologies or systems.

ISSN: 1466-9455

Published by Stairwell Books

ISBN: 978-1-917334-21-1

Contents – Authors

Featured Artist *Kimbal Bumstead*	1
Editorial	3
In Conversation with … Ralph Dartford	5
Hope's Eve *Ralph Dartford*	12
The Wrong 'uns *Ralph Dartford*	14
Basildon 1972 *Ralph Dartford*	15
Poem in Which I Attempt to Adequately Explain Medicine *Tom Ratcliffe*	16
The Victoria and Albert Ward, London, 2003 *Tom Ratcliffe*	18
Hospital Grounds *Shaun Barr*	19
Breathing *Barbara Howerska*	20
Baby Shower *Jane Newberry*	21
Raccoons *Laura Reanna Smith*	22
Successive Anastomosis of Navelcords *Clare Starling*	23
Catch *Carolyn Oulton*	24
Hoolie *Laura Reanna Smith*	25
The Welsh Have 327 Words for Rain *Phil Knight*	27
Carcassonne *Jean Atkin*	29
Vall D'uxo *Jean Atkin*	29
Memory Lane *Denise Bennett*	30
George Shiras, 'Grandfather Flash', 1893 *Adam Strickson*	31
Lion Teeth *Craig Martin Getz*	32
Old Man's Beard *Wilf Deckner*	33
Nothing Left to Declare *Wilf Deckner*	34
Non-Sens Unique *D G Herring*	35
How You Might Live Among the Dead *Kristina Diprose*	37
The Wind Beats Me as If Someone Might Steal Me Away *Kat Couch*	38
Lost and Found *Shaun Barr*	40
Of Dogs and Horses *Rosie Jackson*	41
Someone Who Knew Her Well	42
Vacant Possession, No Upward Chain *Stuart Handysides*	46
Dedication *Sarah J Bryson*	47
The Ottomans *Phil Vernon*	48
Slicing Sourdough *David Olsen*	49

Bread and Butter *Lauren K. Nixon*	50
Defined *Tom Vaughan*	51
Paper Trail Ann Preston *Ann Preston*	52
9 April 1946 *Ann Preston*	55
Ghost Child *Cosmo Goldsmith*	56
Spirit Goose *Paul Bavister*	57
Snow Geese *Jack Granath*	58
Let Me Tell You a Story *Helen Scadding*	59
We See You, Mr Owl *Tom Ratcliffe*	60
Pigeon *Charles Lomas*	61
Warblers *Connie Greig*	62
Israeli Landscape *Dave Wynne-Jones*	63
After Seeing David Smith's 15 Medals for Dishonor *Annie Kocur*	64
You Gallant Few *Clifford Liles*	65
Pinay Honey Ko *Christopher Webster*	66
Xenophobia *Mark Pearce*	67
Island *Martin Reed*	69
The Gaul *Angela Brodie*	70
Song of the Alley *Pamela Coren*	72
Something or Nothing	73
Fragments of Blue *Lisa Falshaw*	74
The Art of Concealment *Louise Worthington*	75
An Equal Music *Rosie Jackson*	76
Miracle *Andrew Senior*	77
The Twilight Bus, the Last of Its Kind, Has Long Gone *Simon French*	78
The Heart-Shackles Are Not as You Think *Clare Bryden*	79
Housework *Jet McDonald*	81
Acts of Devotion *Elaine Ewart*	82
This Won't Change Things *Elaine Ewart*	83
Les Goûts *Charles Lomas*	85
The Sound *Tom Vaughan*	86
The Light Switch Moment *Cathryn M. Spiller*	87
The Ruins of Lowestwood Mill, No Soundtrack *Adam Strickson*	88
Stained *Lauren K. Nixon*	89
Self Portrait *Rachel Goodman*	90
Another Self Portrait *Andria Jane Cooke*	91
Nude Models *David Sapp*	92

South Facing *Claire Booker*	94
Automat *John Scarborough*	95
But I Diverge – a Ghazal *Clare Starling*	96
Shadow Bees *Paul Bavister*	97
Mourning the Queen *Heather Deckner*	98
Time on the Doorstep *Richard Smith*	99
Planted *Lisa Falshaw*	101
Everyday *Marius Grose*	102
Ash *Shaun Barr*	103
Dejà Vu *Andrew Pearson*	104
The Man in the Clock *Martin Reed*	105
Jenga *Andrew Pearson*	106
Two Drunks, One Park Bench, New York City, 1984 *Annie Kocur*	107
Étude 60 *Ray Malone*	109
Normal for Selby *Greg Forshaw*	110
The Luthier's Gift *Jane Newberry*	114
Now the Church is in a Blaze *Adam Strickson*	115
Polymorphous Perversity Bach *Charles Lomas*	116
Morendo *David Olsen*	117
Folk in Tune *Simon Tindale*	118
Audience to Comic *Pamela Coren*	119
St Pancras' Well *Heather Deckner*	120
Tow Rope *John Scarborough*	121
On Omaha Beach *Angela Brodie*	122
Summer Evening Parents *Richard Smith*	124
Cabin Bed *Clare Starling*	125
Undercurrent *Sarah J Bryson*	126
Catch a Wave *Keith Willson*	127
Hokusai's Great Wave at the Hammersmith Flyover *Marius Grose*	128
A Conversation with a Pillar Holding Up the M32 Motorway (junction 2) *Jet McDonald*	129
Crush *Simon French*	131
The Peaceful Transfer of Power *Tom Ratcliffe*	132
In Parliament *Pamela Coren*	133
One Basket *Elaine Ewart*	134
The Lift *Dave Foxton*	136
Six Prints *Barbara Howerska*	137

Dream of a Son *Jennifer Harrison* 138
The Good Worker *Paul Brownsey* 140
Hazel Time *Angela Brodie* 146
Pas De Deux 147
Dietary Changes of the Woke Generation *Sue Spiers* 151
Herdwick Ram *Claire Booker* 152
The Lamp Room *Ian Chapman* 153
Between the Covers *Claire Booker* 158
To a Spider *Keith Willson* 159
Fly Trap *Clare Starling* 160
Fiendish *Nick Cooke* 161
Editors *Dave Wynne-Jones* 163
Wildfires *Simon French* 164
REVIEWS 165
Dancing About Architecture, Edited by Oz Hardwick and Cassandra Atherton *Hannah Stone* 165
Diverted to Split by Hugh McMillan *Nick Allen* 166
Strange Husbandry by Lorcán Black *Patrick Lodge* 167
New and Selected Poems by Paul Sutherland *Hannah Stone* 169
Exit Strategy by Patrick White *Nick Allen* 171
Kindling by Julie Burke *Pauline Kirk* 172
Miniskirts in the Waste Land by Pralibha Castle *Pauline Kirk* 172
Index of Authors 175

Featured Artist
Artist Statement: Kimbal Bumstead

Journeys are better if the person making the journey knows that, to quote the American philosopher Ralph Waldo Emerson, it's not about the destination, it's about the journey. Such pleasing platitudes intersect with poetry all the time. Self-help, mindfulness, and positive hashtags are all healthy by-products of taking journeys, writing poems about journeys, and even repeating cliches about journeys. It's the surrender to the story as it is being written that is perhaps more liberating than closing the final page of the book. The screen-goes-black fate of TV mob boss Tony Soprano is eternally ambiguous, a blow to those who demand closure in their stories, but perfectly in line with his equivocal arc, and indeed the JukeBox song he selects in the final scene, Journey's (who else?) *Don't Stop Believin'*. Virginia Woolf's Mrs Ramsay luxuriates in the freedom of the Shakespeare sonnet she reads whilst her husband sits opposite and silently judges her: unlike him, she is not a philosopher, and unlike him she eschews intellectual analysis to enjoy the freedom the poem:

> "And then there it was, suddenly entire, shaped in her hands, beautiful and reasonable, clear and complete, the essence sucked out of life and held rounded here: the sonnet."

The academic meaning of the sonnet may elude but the exploration of it thrills.

It is this free fall into Art that brings us to the latest collection by UK painter, Kimbal Bumstead. At times pulsing like phosphorescence, with luminous arabesques offset by playful plains of colour and wriggling, vivid marks, Kimbal's irrepressible mischief seems to stem from his striving rather than arriving. He obviously hopes the viewer is along for the ride too.

"The subject matter isn't fixed, it's yet to be defined," says Kimbal. "If the idea of journeying is the building block of the painting, the overarching theme is, I think, that there's no destination. I love the process of trying to let go and getting lost in the painting. That's a positive to me, and reflects on how I live my life. Stuff happens, you navigate it, and hopefully you enjoy the process. I like trying to see a street differently each time I walk down it, and the same goes for my paintings – each time I look at them I find something new, something I hadn't noticed before."

It is the process, then, that provides the flame within both the creation of art and the consumption of it. The shifting, liquid light of Kimbal Bumstead's art is testament to this truth, as are many of the poems held in this very issue. Mary Oliver's 'The Journey' is perhaps the ultimate poetic touchstone:

and there was a new voice
which you slowly
recognized as your own,
that kept you company
as you strode deeper and deeper
into the world,
determined to do
the only thing you could do –
determined to save
the only life you could save.

And then there's The Office's Andy Bernard: "I wish there was a way to know you're in the good old days before you've actually left them."

Poetry, painting, and platitudes. Here's to a great issue and a bright journey.

Greg McGee

PAGES OF ARTWORK

Love	*Cover*
The Fortune Teller	26
The Dealer	54
Circle	80
Coffee and Cigarettes	108
Under the Lea	135

Editorial

This time last year I had just finished teaching an Open University module which included among its themes 'continuity and change.' This polarity crops up regularly in my ruminations about our national and global plight – and seemed to preoccupy contributors to this issue of Dream Catcher. The Dream Catcher community marked the 'continuity' of fifty issues with a fine celebration in Leeds earlier this year; previous editors attended, including our founder Paul Sutherland (whose *New and Selected* poems features in our review pages). Who knows what changes we will also face, as we launch into issue 51, 52, 53 ...? By way of continuity, my 'conversation with' features again a fine poet who has many strings to his bow, Ralph Dartford: I hope you find his insights as engaging as I did.

A record number of poems in DC 51 seem to be 'after' (not in the sense of chronology, but infused or prompted by some other work – I blame Napowrimo). To quote Billy Collins, 'The trouble with poetry' is 'that it encourages the writing of more poetry.' Other writers, works of art, historical and life events have all inspired the contributions included here. Only in DC 51 will you meet drunks slumped on a bench in New York, an Obijwe hunter, the drowned sailors of a fishing boat, join in a conversation with a pillar holding up a motorway bridge, learn how to live among the dead, admire renaissance painting and engage with a fifteen century Scottish maker.

Since antiquity, writers have riffed on how to make art which is new but also engages with subjects and experiences of perennial interest. Can we find fresh ways to express the eternal? Heraclitus claimed that no man ever steps in the same river twice, for it is neither the same river nor the same man (and if you are unconvinced by the agency of rivers, I refer you to Robert Macfarlane's latest book, *Is A River Alive?*). And so our stories and poems in DC 51 reveal that as time passes we may change, but we retain the desire to share ideas and to explore ways of 'telling it slant.' It is always a delight to sift through the submissions and find the works that startle, grab your attention, provoke an 'ah, yes!' And each of the editorial team has particular tastes and desiderata, which we hope makes for a diverse whole.

Jean Rhys saw all writing as 'a huge lake', fed by 'great rivers' such as Tolstoy or Dostoevsky, to which she contributed her 'mere trickles'. She felt that 'all that matters is feeding the lake'. This articulation of creativity as a shared enterprise is quoted in the eponymous monthly online poetry journal published by John Murphy. So I invite you to channel Billy Collins and

'sit in the dark and wait for a little flame
to appear at the tip of [your] pencil.'

As I know all too well, it can be discouraging not to have your work accepted, so I would urge you to persevere, to work at the craft of your poetry (I appreciate Ralph's frankness about this aspect of how his work has grown); to find the place where your work fits. And, to quote the Fran Lock 'Poem in which I attempt to adequately explain my process' which framed our stunning opener by Tom Ratcliffe this time, to do it 'again and again and again'.

Hannah Stone

In Conversation With ... Ralph Dartford

HS: Thanks so much, Ralph, for being my guest in 'the editor in conversation with' feature for Dream Catcher. As with my previous guests, your creative output is so much more than just writing poetry, and I'd like to touch on the many dimensions of your work in our chat.

RD: My pleasure; I am happy to share my journey and explain how important it is to me that I foster creativity in those I encounter in various writing communities.

HS: It is well known that writing about recovery from addiction is a major theme in your work, and in your collections *Recovery Songs*, *Hidden Music* and *House Anthem* this is one of the topics that shapes the poems; the titles also suggest, however, that music has been crucial in your process not only of self-healing but also of translating trauma into art. Can you say a little more about addiction and music, as catalysts to your work?

RD: From an early age, before I could really read, I listened to music and songs, especially the lyrics that inhabit within the walls of a song, its melody and rhythm. It was my escape route out of a severely dyslexic childhood. I left school without a single qualification and little confidence. The only way that I had any relevance was to mask my deficiency by showing off to others and to lose myself in music and art. I managed to get accepted into a local college in Essex on the performing arts course and that really lit the torch for me. I was quite a good actor and alongside that – through necessity – I became a good reader (but a slow one). I got accepted into the big drama schools in London with the view of becoming a professional actor but it was unaffordable for my parents, and I could not get a grant to support me. However, my tenacity led me to get backstage jobs in West End theatres and began a lengthy career working in theatres and eventually to a prominent level whereby I managed the Bloomsbury Theatre at UCL (University College London). That is where the real problems started because due to my high profile, I began mixing with the wrong kind of showbiz people and this is when an addiction to substances and alcohol started.

HS: So, at this stage, the concept of stage performance, which was to become a crucial part of your work, preceded getting published; these were the first skills you honed?

RD: Yes, you could say that; performance poetry with the collective I managed once I moved to Yorkshire (A Firm of Poets) was a springboard, although the pressure of the success with that, especially touring, made me unwell again; it was a real yoyo. While still in London I benefitted from the fact that UCL encouraged their staff to undertake further education which they would pay for. I found I was good at writing; took a course in poetry at Birkbeck College under the tutelage of the great Michael Donaghy. I fell deeply in love with poetry and did very well there.

HS: Tell me how you came to be published for the first time.

RD: I'd run away to Yorkshire to try and free myself from deepening addiction issues, and here I have been for 20 years. I got well, then unwell, then well again etc. A lot of people got hurt by my behavior and it has taken years to make amends to them, and reparation will be an ongoing eternal process. Eventually on the advice of professionals, I walked away from performance and tours and concentrated on my recovery and writing about my experience. I listened to so much music. Out of that period came my first collection *Recovery Songs* which also turned into a show that went on tour. I was worried about performing again because of the stresses and temptations that could potentially bring, but I surrounded myself with good people and it was a success both artistically, and more importantly personally. My recovery became inextricably linked with the reading and writing of poetry as the most important things in my life. The continuing success of that first collection is wonderful and I have great affection for it. I still read poems from the book and run numerous workshops in prisons on the themes of the book. My subsequent collections are technically better, but *Recovery Songs* still carries a tangible impact.

HS: Was there a shift in mood when you came to write your second collection; was there a danger you could just be known as 'the Recovery Poet'? And what types of music nourish your writing?

RD: Absolutely; with *Hidden Music*, I wanted to write something completely different, and to show development in technique and form. I was listening to music that meant something to me, not necessarily my favorite music, but music that caused a reaction in me. I started writing poems that 'jumped off' the music and told stories. It was a deeply fulfilling writing experience for me. Of course, there are poems about recovery in the collection, I will never escape that, but there are narrative stories in the collection that I wouldn't have been able to write without being inspired by the source music that amazes me: songs such as Elvis Costello's 'Shipbuilding', Pulp's 'Common People' and Nick Cave's 'Jesus Alone'. The book was published during Covid which limited my opportunities to do readings of the work which was frustrating. Whenever I do a reading now, I ensure I always read poems from the collection. Some of my favorite poems are in there. The political, personal, spiritual and flights of fancy.

HS: Your most recent collection is different again, and I understand it changed shape even as you wrote it?

RD: Yes, *House Anthems* came as an unintentional surprise to me. I was working in a 'Bail Hostel' in Leeds as a 'Writer in Residence'. I enjoyed it very much to the point where I became a full-time support worker helping men who have been released from prison on license. This meant working long overnight shifts where nothing much happened, which gave me time to write. I had been contracted to write a third collection and was keen to write about contemporary England. The collection was going well but then something catastrophic happened, my younger brother Joseph died suddenly in complicated circumstances and this tragedy flipped the collection. The book is still about England but seen through the eyes of both my brother and me. It is a book about mourning, love, and anger: the collection opens with a long contextual introduction. Again, music is important and there is even a playlist of songs to accompany each poem. I've also recorded a musical album of the poems with Basildon school friend, Gary Clark, available in all digital formats, which we have performed at festivals – a deeply satisfying experience and something I never really expected.

HS: Was this collaboration with a musician a one off?

RD: I have collaborated with musicians before, jazz quartets and folk musicians. I have great memories of one of my poems being set to music by composer Ed Cooper and sung by the wonderful Jacqui Wicks for the Leeds Lieder Festival. It was one of the most extraordinary things I have ever been involved in.

HS: I'm so pleased to hear that; facilitating the poets-composers forum for Leeds Song (as it is now called) is one of the great joys of my poetry life within the community. Can we talk about how you use poetry with offenders: it seems to be sadly the case that people who suffer from addiction may also be drawn into the criminal justice system, and I believe that among the many varied jobs you have had, staffing a bail hostel has been a pivotal one, and that you have also taught creative writing in prison. Can you say something about the contribution made by poetry and art in general on people whose physical liberty has been confined?

RD: I have been able to draw on my own experiences of addiction and recovery when working with offenders, and in particular I find sharing the poems in Recovery Songs works well when I'm running workshops for prisoners who themselves are struggling with addiction and whose crimes encourage substance dealing and associated activity. Working in the Bail Hostel in Leeds as a writer has indeed been pivotal to my career. There, I worked with men who had committed serious crimes. The opportunity given to them to be creative allowed them to look at themselves, to reflect and see the world differently. To be selfish, it allowed me look at society in a separate way: to try and understand a broken criminal justice system caused by poverty (the recruiter of crime) which leads to severe mental illness and cruelty. Above all, it taught me about myself: that I am flawed and sometimes frightened in this world (that we all perhaps are) and that to show vulnerability and empathy is something not to hide, but to express in a vital way of living a fulfilling, caring and purposeful life.

I really loved doing the work at the hostel and this led me to being employed by the National Literacy Trust to work as a Project Manager within their Criminal Justice team teaching and facilitating in the prisons, working with men with low literacy levels and concentrating on how to release their creativity. It is very different from the Bail Hostel in terms of environment. The prison system is archaic and mean, aimed at punishment and not rehabilitation or learning. To me, this is a terrible crime against humanity. People are put into prison for committing crimes and some of these crimes are profoundly serious and the public must always be protected in the first instance. But most prisoners who serve a sentence return to prison repeatedly because rehabilitation is nonexistent as a form of a deterrent.

HS: So you believe that running creative writing workshops in prison can form part of the rehabilitation which should be provided to offenders? Is it possible to *teach* creativity or is it rather a matter of fostering the circumstances which are conducive to it?

RD: I really believe that by teaching creativity, we give the opportunity for criminals to explore themselves, to take a breath and think about the abstract and alternatives. I bring in guest writers such as poets, rappers, novelists, children's writers, podcaster and songwriters, to get the incarcerated men talking, reading, and writing on many subjects. Sometimes the results are astonishing and sometimes chaotic. We see men create absolute brilliance and a sense of positive otherness, sometimes we just eat biscuits and get shouted at. At its best and for 2 hours a week their imaginations are let off the leash and their situations are at the very least alleviated through creativity. When we write or read in the workshop sessions, we try to concentrate on themes that are outside crime or the individual's prison experience. This was a risk because it is sometimes perceived that prisoners would only respond to themes that mirror their own lived experience. Far from it, the last thing that a prisoner wants to write, read, or talk about is their crimes and their life inside. I have honestly seen and heard work that is publishable, restorative and heartbreaking once creativity is given free reign. The job is shattering. I and many other creatives leave the prisons exhausted, sometimes in tears and sometimes in elation, but personally, I do not regret a single day trying to change something, however tiny that impact is perceived on the outside. I know it can be huge.

HS: It must be fantastic to know you are making such a difference, using poetry as a medium for all of that. Can we move to think about another dimension of your output; how the words work off the page? Given your experience in theatre and podcasting etc, is there a sense for you that there is a relationship between what the words sound like dynamically and how they might be captured in the more static context of printing?

RD: When I wrote *Recovery Songs* it was initially for performance. It was written over a short period and with urgency, and sometimes little attention to form. They are written to be heard in the first instance and read afterwards. The collection works in its direction, I think. Some of the poems are lyrical in terms of storytelling and are conversational in style. It has subsequently become important to me that a poem works equally well on the page and aurally. This is something that has become an overriding ambition to me, and I strive to find the intersection between the page and performance. After *Recovery Songs* I realized that I wanted to become a poet who understood form and technique. I enrolled in the master's program at Sheffield Hallam University and was lucky to work with great poets and technicians such as Chris Jones and Harriet Tarlo and they encouraged me to read extensively; two of the most important poets for me are Phillip Larkin and Seamus Heaney. Through repeated reading, I learned from them how a poem should look and sound. Their respective techniques make me gasp in wonderment – Larkin for discipline and Heaney for lyrical trapeze acts. I highly recommend Glynn Maxwell's *On Poetry* and Ruth Padel's *52 Ways of Looking at a Poem*, Glynn's for how a poem looks and feels on the page, and Ruth's for how a poem is broken down, read forensically, and how it sounds.

With my second collection, *Hidden Music*, there is a concentrated effort on form and sound. I wanted the poems to sing lyrically. I use 'sound echoes' to drive a poem, and rhyme and half rhyme in an effort for the reader to take on the next line, to hold their interest. Line breaks and run on sentences have also become important to me for quickening up and slowing down a poem and how a poem is mapped on a page; these techniques are developed further in *House Anthems*.

HS: What are you working on now, and how does it differ from your first three collections?

RD: I've begun writing a fourth collection titled, *The Wrong'uns* which is a departure for me, as it is a novel in verse. At the heart of the collection there are three connected 'working class' protagonists who reveal the tale of their lives. Two of these are named Terry and Julie, and they are the couple based on the characters from the famous Ray Davies 1960's pop song, *Waterloo Sunset*. The third protagonist is their unnamed son who works within the criminal justice system as a teacher of creative writing in prisons. The poetic form techniques that will be deployed in the collection vary from the lyrical tradition: balladry, villanelle, sonnets and some of these techniques will be subverted to reflect modern poetic trends. There will also be poems that work as 'free verse' and 'prose poems. The aim of the collection is to entertain and move the reader. Additional to this, the collection hopes to encourage people to evaluate the consequences of their own lives regardless of what stage of that life they are at. It's going to be quite a challenge but one that I relish.

HS: We're delighted to be publishing some of these in this issue of Dream Catcher. Moving to another matter, your editorship of Northern Gravy is perhaps your most well-known contribution to the poetry community; publication in that ezine is a hotly contested achievement, not least as you have ensured that poets are PAID for their contributions, a very rare situation. Can you tell us about the genesis of Northern Gravy, its ethos and ongoing projects – I am excited that you will be publishing a series of anthologies of writing (including poems and prose) under that imprint with Yorkshire based Valley Press.

RD: *Northern Gravy* is a project involving children's writer, Jonny Syer, fiction writer, Nick Jones, and me; we were fellow students at Sheffield Hallam University. We're now in our third year of publishing new writing. The aim was to keep us involved in literature after we graduated and to be present and active within the landscape. *Northern Gravy* was a way of us being a part of it. It was very important to us those writers should be paid for their work and not just give it away for the prestige of being published. Literature has a value as an art form, and we wanted to be clear on that. Also, by paying people, we knew that we would attract high quality writers who would really think about the work they submitted. We receive over 1000 submissions per edition and it's a joy to read such brilliant work. We can only publish twelve pieces per edition because of our financial commitments (we are funded by the Arts Council England), so decision making is tough. We wish we could publish more.

We are producing physical anthologies later this year with the wonderful *Valley Press* and we are excited about that. The books will reflect all the writing from the first two years of *Northern Gravy*. They will hopefully be on sale in the summer, and we will be running events to celebrate their launch.

HS: I am really looking forward to getting my copy – it was a huge thrill when you accepted my work for Northern Gravy. Somehow in your busy life you have managed to fit in studying for a PhD in Creative writing, under the direction of Steve Ely; I believe the focus of this is on working class poetry. Tell us more!

RD: Yes. I'm doing my PhD at Huddersfield with Steve. He has become a good friend and a fantastic supervisor. I'm about halfway through now. My practice concerns itself with working class poetry of the 21st century, its overreliance on performance rather than the page, why that happens, and does that harm the aesthetic tradition of poetry that is written to be read? I'm trying to find the perfect intersection between the page and performance, and that will hopefully reflect in the poetry collection I submit. I'm not trying to incite poetry riots for an age-old argument but attempting to find the best response for me that might inspire others. I've discovered that there is not a right or wrong answer to my provocation, just an informed opinion.

HS: We wish you well with that, and look forward to seeing the completed collection and meanwhile, thanks for sharing your truly inspirational insights with us in Dream Catcher.

RD: You're welcome.

Hope's Eve

Dirty old river
must you keep rolling
beneath a setting sun
for the boy who waits ...

Mod suited, Chelsea booted
outside the Friday night hum
of trains traversing this way ...
               ... and trains conversing that way.

This boy.
He knows these arteries.
The tides and the tracks
of London's bloodlines.
He can count the pulsed veins.

As he stands, he is so wondrous
that he puffs on two Strand
cigarettes, sucks on a Trebor
mint and considers his tie.

And then again,
considers his tie.

When she finally appears
on the station steps, French
cropped, Mary Quant propped,
she is determined – a little shy.

Her first step
in monochrome,
her second sepia,
her third Technicolor,
her fourth a kissed embrace
that forces the faces
of Big Ben to blush to a bow.

The jealous flower shop girls
of Waterloo scatter petals as they
walk to their cul-de-sacs of Kennington,
weeping into petticoats and singing
solo in a blue weekend swoon.

Their moments will surely come …

But not tonight.
This Friday night
is the 30th of July.
1966.

Hope's Eve.

Tomorrow, a Russian linesman
will wink at Bobby Moore launching
Jules Rimet into a skidding Wembley sky.
Harold Wilson of Huddersfield
will finger his pipe and smile at it all.

And right here, now.
Inside this pub underneath
the cooling railway arches.
Over pints of Watney's Pale Ale
and chipped glasses of Babycham –
Terry and Julie sparkle into each
other's eyes for the very first time.

Later, they will walk by that river,
talking in tongues until the dawn breaks
over Tower Bridge and a raven's croak.

For an old England in new rags.

Ralph Dartford

THE WRONG 'UNS
(after 'V' by Tony Harrison)

'My father still reads the dictionary every day. He says your life depends on your power to master words.' Arthur Scargill, *The Sunday Times*, 10 Jan. 1982

And I love the men and I've asked God
for the reasons why. There has been no answer.
Perhaps it's a case of quandary or of abidance.
These men. They have the rage to kill me –
their wives, children, friends, each other.

I walk into their rooms with paper and pens.
Shaking their hands, slapping their backs.
We talk football, the structure of a sonnet,
court dates, plot devices. How to make blades.
I sit by the door as all the training dictates.

But it's too late to run away from all this now.
I've looked into their eyes and seen the madness
reflecting between us. The loneliness of wrong.
Sometimes I'm convinced of our redemption.
But who are we conning? Push becomes punch.

Later in the chapel. I sit and read their poems.
I say my prayers and wait for the answers to come.
Their rhymes of mat, cat, and rat. Son and gun.
   Sonnets have a structure and a law of iambic rhythm.
   All Gods are jangling keys here. Ignoring the unforgiven.

Ralph Dartford

BASILDON 1972

Those new town early years.
Pushchairs, lollipops, and wasps.
Paths, treeless streets, and coughs.
The colours of weakened beer.

Everywhere our footprints on carpets.
The mustard sand on kaleidoscope trickling
down the sides of sofas, peppering the bedsheets
and gritting tide marks to our baths, our saucepan hats.

The Thalidomide kid who was good in goal.
A cap and khaki war hero whistling on his bike.
60 a day Jack – his 'Battle of Cable Street' fists.
Liver for tea, Liver for tea, Liver for tea.

Ralph Dartford

Poem in Which I Attempt to Adequately Explain Medicine
(After Fran Lock)

Poem in which I walk into the resuscitation room,
see the feet of a dead child, candle white.

Poem in which A&E is a supermarket checkout,
people bagged up, led to cars, wheeled to wards,
next please, and on it goes.

Poem in which we move Becky's notes to the top of the pile,
so she can get home to die. She is thirty-four.

Poem in which a dead child is a cold, hard, fact.
Tears can wait. Here, there is work to be done.

Poem in which nurses and trainee docs do twelve-hour night shifts
on the living wage, jam, toast and tea.

Poem in which you tell the surgeon you don't want your appendix out,
so he pulls the sheet over your face, tells you *to go and fucking die.*

Poem in which I hear you unzip your bag in the waiting room,
but I dare not look inside.

Poem in which I look inside.

Poem in which the evil things your parents did re-wired your mind,
now everything hurts, despite everything we try.

Poem in which we hold your wasted hand and cry together.
There is just morphine and cups of tea.

Poem in which a 20-year-old alcoholic exsanguinates
through his mouth and rectum. We can only watch.

Poem in which your cupboards are full of pills, prescribed with care,
that you have not taken.

Poem in which we are taught we must pronounce diagnoses
like a Pope speaking *ex cathedra*.

Poem in which power and status always get in the way.

Poem in which we reduce everything to acronyms, search
for answers in a flow chart, emerge empty handed.

Poem in which some days we have finite fucks to give.

Poem in which the Department for Health tells you every symptom could be cancer.

Poem in which we rant about time wasters and the worried well.

Poem in which we diagnose acute leukaemia, and save a child's life, in which we miss a heart attack, and a man dies.

Poem in which this glorious folly is better than nothing.

Poem in which it doesn't matter anymore, we just need to go home.

Tom Ratcliffe

The Victoria and Albert Ward, London, 2003

These were the stroked-out birds of The Blitz
tucked with military order into beds, laid out
in rows, too weak to ruffle their nylon sheets.

Gran is going on about the war again!
Stories on repeat: rationing, air raids, V2s,
dreaded telegrams. And no-one is listening.

They never failed to thank the staff, never grumbled.
At night their worlds were shrunk to lamp lit pools,
where frightened children cried out for nurse.

An emptied bed each week. Another chance
to ask *what was it really like* lost.
Then the ward fell silent, before it shut for good.

Tom Ratcliffe

Hospital Grounds

Across white-sheeted lawns
and the scattered ghosts
of maple leaves
frosted where they fell

the sun is stretching shadows
from skeletal trees,
bare but for the berries
the birds have left.

Winter thick in our lungs
we circle the grounds without speaking,
refuged in the silence of things frozen;
words as lost as we are.

Shaken by the shock of the expected
we cling to the arm of routine
as if life depended on it,
watch the daily walk turn into swansong.

Stopping at the turned-off fountain
we stare at the stranded coins;
see how useless the currency of hope is:
thrown at what we cannot bear.

Shaun Barr

Breathing

While l was away
breathing.
The windscreen wipers sent
me gifts.
The first, a bunch of crocodile tears
disguised as Orange Gerbera,
their soft green stems
bending under the weight of gravity.

The second was a book of egos.
Black with knife-sharp ribbon wrapped around it.
The words inside
were
jumping and down like angry little monkeys.

But I was busy
watching the leaf-like, curling patterns,
of windowed shadows dancing on the wall,
thrown up from car headlights.

Silent in the grey
milky light of the hospital ward.

Barbara Howerska

BABY SHOWER
illumine: verb, light up; enlighten spiritually.

Silent ultrasound beam
pierces her dark world
and I hold my breath, watching
where the tiny being floats
perfectly illumined in death.

Wrapped in my long sadness
I bring you the light you can never see,
the muted apricot light
we planned for your arrival,
sunlight filtering through apple leaves
where your pram would have been,
sunbeams bouncing off a sunhat
and sea glints inviting your curled toes

I bring you starlight through the window
on a sleepless teething night
and a glow from the bunny nightlight
that we kept anyway.
And as I throw away the gift wrap,
I may light a candle …
for you, just for a little while,
were the light of my life.

Jane Newberry

Raccoons

Only a handful of women
will understand what it's like
to desperately dig
         the
         test
back out the bin
because even though it was negative
45 minutes ago
someone's friend somewhere
had a cousin
who had a sister
whose test turned positive
a few hours later

and while we have no   dignity
we still have shreds
         of
         hope

Laura Reanna Smith

SUCCESSIVE ANASTOMOSIS OF NAVELCORDS
(a duplex after James Joyce)

There are some things the human mind cannot contain –
the circular stapler that joined my intestines.

It joined me up, that inconceivable stapler
via deft science, through the keyhole of my navel.

Through the keyhole of my navel, my morphine dreams
led me back up the umbilical cord phone line.

I made a call, back up the umbilical line – my mother,
grandmother, great-grandmother answered.

All the lost grandmothers, singing, smocking, swelling,
babies clinging to their long hair, swimming in the sea.

Swimming and smiling in the wild sea, gazing up,
bubbles of air in body hair, primal mouths agape –

Mouths agape, puzzling at the circling stars:
there are some things the human mind cannot contain.

Clare Starling

Catch

That sound is deep in the wind
as it struggles up and falls again.
The wood has felt rain
growing between its feet
until the path is soggy, slumping
like pastry under its weight.

The earth is gulping leaves
too fast to swallow, most
are lying around half-chewed.
Those colours in the sky
are disconnected, sure
to topple any moment now.

I get it full in the eye. Light
pushing the clouds. Flint
sculpted the way lines drag
across a rough-edged sea.
God laughing, holding trouble
just beyond my reach.

Carolyn Oulton

HOOLIE

The wind of the Highlands
didn't gently tousle my hair
it grabbed me by the shoulders
knotted its frozen fingers through my chest
and held out my bloody heart before me

Do yer still want this?
it called
spitting rain in my face
red dripping down its wrist

My reply came
on the fog-licked cairn of Ben Nevis
gulped between the cold slaps of Durness waves
skimmed on the warm Black Isle sunset
scratched out by Sheildaig's stars
shouting for attention
on the way back from washing up

It was glinting on the Storr's ragged blade
stretching across the unbrushed vastness
brutal and beautiful
damp and unruly

It came in the native tongue
of seals and otters
and indignant sheep
who don't owe you a road

Yes
I nod
I still want it
now I'm here

Laura Reanna Smith

The Fortune Teller

The Welsh Have 327 Words for Rain

3 Aberavon
Rain that tastes of salt, carbon and despair.

21 Aberystwyth
Rain that comes at you horizontally from the sea
and goes up your sleeve past your wristwatch.

49 Blaenafon!
Rain that hits the ground with such force it shoots up
your leg and you cry out in surprise: BLAENAFON!

55 Caerleon
Rain that is like a fine mist which clings to the day
like an ancient shroud.

62 Crickhowell
Rain so cold it makes your every joint ache.

91 Doluaucothi
Rain that makes stones and roads gleam like
burnished gold.

104 Eisteddfod
Rain that returns every year without failure or surprise.

157 Lampeter
Rain that stops and starts and stops and starts etc, etc.

166 Llandaff
Rain that makes your hair sticky.

203 Margam
Rain of classic cinema funerals.

227 Merthyr Tydfil
Rain that pours even when the sun is shining.

244 Neath
Rain that falls perfectly vertically and gets beneath
your vest.

277 Ponterdawe
Rain that has an almost musical cadence.

301 Swansea
Rain so heavy you cannot see where you are going.

327 Ystradgnlais
Rain that makes you nostalgic for the rain of your youth.

Phil Knight

Carcassonne

We're lost. Kind people drive in front of us,
in dusk and rain, to lead us to the campsite.
First light, the *gardien* cuts off the water

before breakfast. He says he is now closed
for winter. We ride off under the ramparts,
without paying, in more rain.

Jean Atkin

Vall D'uxo

Could have been flaking Baroque, but even
in a storm is clearly post-war Fascist.

Blank concrete streets run deep in flood.
In the morning everything is stained with red.

Jean Atkin

MEMORY LANE
i.m. Johnny Kingdom 1939 – 2018

It was gift of a camera,
after his accident,
that changed his life.

He swapped his hunting gun
for a wide-angle lens,
flexing his trigger-finger to shoot

the roe deer grazing at dawn,
the shy badger after dark.
He became a night owl;

built a hide to observe birds,
set up a camera to film them feed,
fledge; penance for his stalking days.

He spoke in schools, took visitors
on Exmoor safaris – and when
he died people lined the lane

like cow parsley to see his coffin pass.
They buried him under the green
folds of a Devon hill.

*I found him under the chestnut tree,
lying by his digger, as if asleep,*
his widow said.

Denise Bennett

GEORGE SHIRAS, 'GRANDFATHER FLASH', 1893

His sleek canoe, whiter than an albino porcupine,
than the tail of that stunned doe pinned
in the jacklight, doped by the brightness,
still as the lake water, candle-eyed.

*

Once

the Obijwe hunter sat on the stern, with his fire
lit in a pan on the prow, prayed, then pulled back
the trigger, aimed right between the beast's eyes
and paddled the corpse home – the butcher's heartsong.

But Ol' Grandfather Flash used a kerosene lamp,
his shutter the release of the trigger, his camera
the gun, his passion the motion-trap, the wild
in white glow, fur-shimmer on glass plates.

Those photos, such *swiftness in repose*,
the reckless leaps of three deer frozen in air,
the pent energy of drawn back hooves,
the cream underbellies caught in the frame.

And so it began, in the glide of that canoe,
the wonder-capture, the other staring back
into lenses: unbridled, haunting nature.
We capture beauty, can't hold back the fire.

Adam Strickson

Lion Teeth

Before all this, my one and only long-lasting love story,
I had grabbed a bunch of dandelions in the northwest of Spain.

Decades later, my mother died in California. The dandelions,
fresh, firm and sunny against a plaid flannel of beige and blue

the second-hand sleeves of which never reached my wrists,
were still there on her fridge; the Atlantic Ocean in the 80s,

me sitting atop some ancient ruins you would never guess
in the autopsy of her home. Years later, with Dad gone too,

and your father too and your mother, we venture, the next
to die, orphans along the Pacific edge, past towns named after

saints, sunsets, cliffs to which the very same weeds cling,
blooming their yellow youth and entrusting their white demise

to onshore winds. And me, forever in the throes of fully
realizing myself in Spanish, a strange language that arrived

one day in pursuit of legends of gold, of silver, and worried
about the hereafter of souls, I ask you but you don't know

the name of the flowers; and I let it go, *dientes de león*,
giving it little importance, until today.

Craig Martin Getz

OLD MAN'S BEARD
'And summer's green all girded up in sheaves,
Borne on the bier with white and bristly beard'
(William Shakespeare: Sonnet XII)

An old man's beard, stubble bleached silver,
Framing my face, sparse thistledown on top,
A dandelion clock after St. Martin's summer,
Can only partially conceal the living skull,
Much closer now to the attenuated surface,
Above a wrinkled neck, corded with tendons.

Still broad enough in outward semblance,
Shoulders bear evidence of muscles withered,
Where bushy foliage once bolstered shirts,
They're draped around a lean and stringy frame,
Deep hollows behind my collarbones invite
Tendrils and stems of wild clematis to climb up.

Trousers that used to fit, now hang off bony hips
To swathe gaunt contours, my rolled-up sleeves
Exposing forearms, once muscled well enough
To catch her eye, fibrous with rope-like sinews.
The common light of day shows corrugated bark
Spiral from shrunken wrist to blunt-boned elbow.

Even side-on, the desiccation is pronounced,
A ribcage looped with fossilized lianas,
From knotty spine to dry striations marking
A concave abdomen – as palmate pelvis echoes
Angular shoulder blades in a stark symmetry,
Impending winter usurps my dwindling flesh.

Wilf Deckner

NOTHING LEFT TO DECLARE
*'Mortality. They don't reckon with that. Oh, they write poetry about it.
That's another matter.' (Gweneth Lilly: On a Scaffold High)*

My eyes do not condemn what holds their gaze,
The earth I leave is beautiful but wastes no pity
On those, lacking the strength to reach the light.
Although my wish may be to stay, at any age
Between my distant birth and looming end,
Time is a stream that drowns not just the past.

Ceaselessly flowing, its movement irresistible,
A current, shaped to curtail my future with
Lost words that float away, as light as gossamer
Dispersing on the wind, my tangled thoughts,
In wakeful hours of the night, grow near
To choking me, fought each dull-bladed day.

Ahead of me, only the borderland of death,
In whose unfathomable depth all vanishes,
Ambitions or anxieties, love and contempt –
No happiness or grief survives this crossing.
When first I came to it, I harboured hopes,
For what I do not know, since left behind.

Like Pearly Spencer, my race is almost run,
A traveller bereft of joy, each stage of growth
A slow defeat, an open-ended farewell tour,
No 'best before' to show I may have reached
The dark side of the year, self-dramatized
Into a cut-off date, and simply cease to be.

Wilf Deckner

NON-SENS UNIQUE
(From 'Dream of Fair to Middling Women' by Samuel Beckett – punning on the French for 'one-way street' and 'nonsense')
'What am I without you...? A guide to my own downfall...' (Augustine's Confessions)

pouncing
with powder through pinpricks
women etch magical letters
onto their skin before giving
birth

        language
        is the house of being
        Heidegger said   but I speak
        in tongues   lacking the
        key

was it
the acacia tree   lit from
behind by low sun   that spoke
bush and branch   virgin
berth

        Porphyry
        wrote that the generation
        of images in the mind   is like
        water   lapping our feet by the
        quay

        Thomas
        of Chobham thought that
        the force of nature   is inscribed
        in three things   words   herbs
        stone

what
would I be   without you
swimming against the high tide until
two drowned souls become
one

        Wittgenstein
        asked what we mean
        when we say   now
        I know   how   to go
        on

bright
angel   burning up
on re-entry   I will sink   requiescat
in pace   into my tomb-
stone

D G Herring

How You Might Live Among the Dead
(after Wendy Videlock)

like an only child,
like a miracle,
like laughter

at a funeral,
like the apple
of your lover's eye,

like fire,
like sky,
like a light breeze

lifting the curtain,
like the edge
of a dream,

like you
are green
and soft

as fern moss
or tight
as a seed,

like a tide,
like a thief,
like a tongue

on the cusp
of apology,
like an open door,

like you
have never
been here before.

Kristina Diprose

The Wind Beats Me As If Someone Might Steal Me Away

In the mesa winter the cold dry
sews my eyes shut in the night
like an Egyptian mummy's.
I wake four or five times,
legs swung over the bed,
to water them with salt.

Around me are things
I will need in the afterlife:
books of herbs, a notepad,
a brown string with a knot
for the cats I will meet.

New Mexico winds have washed
the packets of my eyes
in cactus tea, the west winds
that edge up along the
Sangre de Cristo mountains.

They have left my eyes
at the top of Culebra Peak
by the gate;
they have been left
at the crossroads
where the big river
inches to Corrales.
They have been left by
the artesian pipe,
by the blue water speedwell,
and they drank and dried,
drank dust and dried.

As I age, the wind does not expect
I will need them, my eyes.
They are soiled with lost love,
the wild foal with the broken leg,
the cartridge that killed summer,
with the burned home.

I have shown you what happens
in the high desert,
the wind from Chama says,

Dream Catcher 51

our own Sirocco,
the Sonoran wind that smells
of ash and creosote:
take our narrowleaf yucca in flower,
cupped like cream in a girl's hands
– by January they're just broken husks
with the black-beetles of seeds.

And you'll remember August,
the pink-lavender tansy aster,
gone to puffballs now.
I have replaced your eyes
with these,
sewed them shut in the night
with thistle-needles and dry linen.

Why are you complaining about
catching up to the pock-marked rock,
the ribbon muscles of piñon,
the dewless topsoil, the clay?

And your lost eyes?

Everything you will need,
the wind says,
is already behind them.

Kat Couch

Note: The title is taken from a quote by Ta-Nehisi Coates: 'My father was so very afraid. I felt it in the sting of his black leather belt, which he applied with more anxiety than anger, my father who beat me as if someone might steal me away, because that was exactly what was happening all around us.'

Lost and Found

I put you in a pocket with a hole in it,
left you in the lining of an overcoat
I knew I would never wear again.

I tucked you into a tiny crevice
at the back of the old church hall where
bats still dream their days away.

I tried to lose you in the blood and bones of me:
an empty room between head and heart,
with the curtains closed.

Then mine-shaft deep I dropped you,
at the bottom of St. Margaret's well;
slab cold and thick with dark.

But waking from a dream in which I'm drowning
in the dead of night you find me,
flailing limbs on soaking sheets.

Then the slow, slow drip of sleepless hours,
as shadows shift across the bedside table,
a sensation of static on skin.

Sometimes I think I hear your voice
and wonder if it might be the ghost of you –
or whether it's just the grief talking.

Shaun Barr

Of Dogs and Horses

You always hated dogs, you wouldn't come back
as one of those.

When your new woman made you look after
her yapping little mongrel, you devised a wire attached to its lead,

        so it could run up and down the yard
alongside yellow sedums (I'd planted), glowing on the wall.

        That was the moment I first knew:
when I found a bag of dog biscuits, hidden under gloves
and scissors in the dresser drawer.

It took a minute, then – *What the fuck?* – I mean, I knew
we didn't have a dog.

She had horses too, you took up riding.
        I fancied driving
to her field to poison one, but I couldn't find her address.
        (The craft shop, where you sold pots
and she sold prints of roses round the door, had been warned.)

        There was one night,
frantic with grief, when I called you – you still in the house
whose curtains I'd made –

and she answered,
        said you were out buying fish and chips –

        that if I was depressed, I should go to the doctor
for help. I asked for you to call back, but you didn't.

        And since you died,
and she got your new house, with field and stables,
I'd still like to meet her –

share with her that dream I sometimes have –
        when you come back, announce it was all a great mistake,
that now you're choosing me over her.

        Then I'll lean on the fence,
see how it fits her,
        that loose saddle of grief.

Rosie Jackson

Someone Who Knew Her Well

"Hello."

"Is that you, Roddy?" The voice is, as always, fragile and doom-laden on the phone, despite the relaxed hedonism with which she lives.

"Alma!" Roddy cries, demonstrating emphatically that he's recognised the voice. Alma won't show she's pleased by this: that wouldn't be her way. Her voice can also sound offhand, sometimes scornful, a voice at odds with her many kindnesses during his mother's illness and death three years ago.

They exchange a few updating words about how they are, and then Alma, who isn't timid, hesitates like someone timid. "What I'm calling about is, well, the thing is, these presents. Someone sending your mother birthday presents. Every year." She seems to wait for his reaction.

"Christ!" he says in an astonished way; perhaps too astonished.

"I didn't know about it until this week. I've agreed to help out at the village shop" – typical Alma, pretending she didn't need a job to support herself as the best-dressed woman in Easterrig, only that she was obliging someone else – "and this man came in and we got talking" – yes, Alma would get talking to a man, all right – "and I realised he was the man of the couple now living in your mother's house and I told him I used to be your mother's friend and he said perhaps I could help them. Every year a birthday present arrives for your mother. They didn't like to throw them out but there was no address they'd come from."

"No." That was silly. "Wasn't there a gift tag with a name?"

"Kit."

"Kit." Musingly.

"Kit."

She's doesn't ask if he knows who Kit could be.

"I never heard of my mother having a friend of that name. I'm sure there was no Kit in her address book, no name like that. I went through it when she died, to let everyone know."

Alma doesn't say, "So there's no way of stopping them arriving."

What she does say is, "The handwriting is little bit like yours, Roddy. From your Christmas cards to me and Len. Don't know if that helps."

He pretends to laugh. "Perhaps she had a secret admirer." That's getting onto Alma's territory, with her history of admirers, some of them not so secret. Once, when she wasn't sure when her husband would be home from the oil rigs, she got Roddy's mother to let the man of the moment stay at his mother's house. Instead of being shocked at being dragged into Alma's shameless love-life, his mother treated it as a lark. He joked with her that Alma was the sort of woman who lounged about all day in black silk pyjamas in case a man called. His mother had laughed like it wasn't her son making that remark and had said, "Any man," so he'd ventured,

Dream Catcher 51

"Maybe I should try that," and she'd laughed again, but not quite in the same way.

Alma ignores his remark about a secret admirer. "I said I knew how to contact Lily's son and I'd take them off their hands and let you have them. They are, well, yours."

"You didn't say what the presents are."

"They're from someone who knew her well."

Roddy waits.

"One of them's perfume, lily-of-the-valley. I once gave her a bottle of Chanel that someone gave me but she wouldn't take it. She said she'd stick to lily-of-the-valley because that was her favourite." Last word emphasised.

"When I was a wee boy," he replies, an anecdote being a safe and sound way to respond, "I used to think it was a rule that she had to use lily-of-the-valley scent because she was called Lily. I'd have expected someone called Rose to use scent smelling of roses. That's how you think when you're a kid. Sometimes I gave it to her for Christmas or her birthday; Yardley's it would be in those days."

"So who would you give Poison to?" There's Alma's scorn, as if she sees his anecdote as blather.

"Poison?"

"It's a perfume."

Another anecdote. "There was a Dior lily-of-the-valley perfume, Diorissimo. I wanted to get her some but it was very expensive. I got a paper round to save up the money, but I was always a sickly child, she wouldn't let me do it, though she actually did it the first week I was due to do it, before she went to work, because she said she didn't want the newsagent let down, and when I told her I wanted the paper round to get her Diorissimno for her Christmas, she said she preferred Yardley's anyway. It didn't occur to me at the time that she wouldn't have known what the Dior stuff smelt like."

"Someone can afford it now."

"It's Diorissimo?"

She takes a while to say, "Yes."

"So what are the other presents?"

"Well, a cassette. That, too – someone who knew her well. It's got a song on it she told me about."

She seems to wait for something.

"Oh?"

"A song called *Little Things Mean A Lot*. She used to talk a lot about how things were when she and you were living with her mother and her mother wasn't very nice at times, she could say hard things, cruel things. 'I wouldn't have minded what I had to put up with if she'd just been nicer,' she'd say, and she said that song always made her cry if she heard it because it always took her back to that time because it was about people being nice, in little things, and your Gran wasn't. But *you* were always nice to her, Roddy." Alma's voice is suddenly warm and generous, somehow of a piece with her dark luxuriant hair he remembers.

"Hey, the presents are from Kit, and Kitty Kallen made that song famous – could that be a clue? Though my mother liked Cliff singing it. Was it Cliff on the cassette?"

Alma doesn't reply.

Roddy says, "So what's the other one?"

There's that pause again. "A little gold cross and chain. The most recent."

He's not afraid of suggesting every possible detail. "Not with, like, little green emeralds on each arm?"

"Don't know about real emeralds." She doesn't ask how he knows. "But green was her favourite colour. Someone who knew her well. Knew that she used to have a little cross like this." He pictures Alma holding it up as she speaks pn the phone.

"She'd never tell me where she got it," Roddy contributes. "'I can have my little secrets,' she'd say. She said it was an antique. I remember she wore it with a green sweater when she had to go to the school to see the headmaster when I was in trouble for reporting a master to the police because of how he punished people. She lost it and was really upset. She said the chain must have broken when she had it on and she didn't realise."

"Well, no, that wasn't it." That's Alma's offhand voice, like what's coming is just a minor correction about something he already knows the gist of, such as what Alma's husband's actually does on the oil rigs. "I don't think you knew your father was married. When he died his wife found letters and tracked your Mum down."

"Right." He managed to keep shock out of the word, and despite his mother telling Alma huge things he didn't know, there's no reason to suppose she'd have told her that when he was a boy his favourite cowboy was Kit Carson and he would buy his adventures every month in the Cowboy Comics series ("64 picture-packed pages") and every year in *Kit Carson's Cowboy Annual*, and sometimes she would say things like, "Come on, Kit, it's half-past seven, time to get up and git rahdin' the range"

Alma is continuing, so casually as to be flattering, "I was having a cup of coffee with her when we saw this woman outside looking at the house, looking all puzzled, and your Mum went out to see if she could help and at first the woman didn't want to say why she was there. Your Mum was wearing the cross with the little green jewels and the woman told her she'd had one just like it but lost it but had never known how, and it was through that that it all came out. Your Mum hadn't known he was married. The man must have stolen it from his wife to give to her. The woman wasn't nasty or anything. And your Mum said she didn't want to keep the cross, knowing it was another woman's, it was the woman's by rights so she gave it back to her."

Dream Catcher 51

"That was so like her. She always used to say, 'Honesty is the best policy – you never suffer by it if you're honest.'"

Alma silence is such a knowing silence.

He says – he's a boy babbling, not a man in his fifties – "Perhaps the cross, the cross that was sent, is, like, the same cross. The woman, his wife, had a change of heart and decided my mother should have it after all."

"You can see her doing that, can you?" Scorn, with the implication he doesn't know a lot about women.

But he tells himself Alma's scorn doesn't go deep, if it's scorn at all, because she can be as nice as pie a moment later. He once said to his mother, "Perhaps being scornful keeps her men on their toes." His mother had given the uninhibited laugh he loved, and Roddy had risked, "Maybe I should try it," and she'd laughed again, but only like someone pretending to laugh.

He's on a stupid line, he knows, but he can't get off it. "Perhaps my mother and the wife kept in contact, wrote to each other, so she could have learned when my mother's birthday was and thought she'd send the cross back to her for her birthday."

"Yeah, even after she got no thanks or anything other years after sending the lily-of-the-valley and the cassette." Then her voice reverts to fragile and doom-laden. "I still miss your Mum, Roddy. Like you do."

"Look, why don't have the little cross, Alma? It would look good on you. Well, you look good in everything. You were a good friend to my mother. She'd be glad for you to have it. A sort of thank you for all you did for her, driving her to her appointments and tests and things. Keeping an eye that her care arrangements worked and the people turned up and so on. And kindnesses to me, too – how you found me crying my eyes out when I got to her house after she died, and took me home and cooked me a meal and got Len to drive me around the next day to see to all the formalities and funeral arrangements. I'll always be so grateful."

"Oh, don't be silly, Roddy. I was glad to." Bashful warmth in her voice; perhaps even a touch of flirtatiousness. Well, this is Alma.

Then: "But it wouldn't feel right, somehow, wearing this cross, the way these things have been coming. From whoever it is."

She doesn't say that it would cause problems if the person who sent them came to Easterrigg looking for Roddy's mother and found Alma wearing the cross. Still, the squeamishness she's expressed is just as much Alma as the black silk pyjamas. "No, I'd rather just pack them up and send them to you, Roddy. I don't expect there'll be any more."

"Why do you think that?" That's what he should have said, he realises after they've said their goodbyes and rung off, but it's not the sort of thing he can phone back to ask.

Paul Brownsey

Vacant Possession, No Upward Chain

Sometimes someone comes to see
the place. They don't stay long.

The water that he left in me remains
long-cooled since he collapsed.

They threw the teabag out
and hung the mug. It swung, and stopped.

The toaster, too, stands cold.
The wheel within the meter hardly moves.

His router was switched off, and no one knew
his passwords: last thoughts left locked up.

They binned the contents of the fridge
and pulled the plug. The puddle has dried out.

The kitchen chairs remain un-sat-upon.
The sometimes chat when I was being filled

and heated, boiled and poured
no longer moves the air about.

It's very quiet now. It was before
but not like this.

Stuart Handysides

DEDICATION

Grandma spent her last year of school
with feather-stitch and smocking,
turning heels of stockings and socks –
three 'r's forgotten. At thirteen she edged
bottom-drawer linen for her teacher's wedding.

She told me this, as she taught me to knit.
She showed me her way to hold the needles
and how to cast on, the difference between plain
and purl, the way to work to make a twisted rib
and the benefit of casting off in loose loops.

She showed me how to hold skeins of freshly washed
wool, unravelled yarn from some outgrown thing
how to wind it into balls ready to use again. A silent
waste not want not. She knitted every spare moment:
constant clicks for birthdays, and new school years

until we grandchildren were out in the world
about the time Grandpa slowed down.
She turned her attention to big-sister him,
as his legs weakened, could not bear his weight.
Towards the end, in the front room, she nursed

his frail body on their displaced double bed,
soft with flannelette sheets and the old eiderdown.
The gas fire for comfort, hissing and clicking,
the knitting needles quiet, laid to rest.

Sarah J Bryson

THE OTTOMANS
(After 'The Ottomans', Mark David Baer, John Murray Press, 2021)

Six hundred years, from nomad clan
to Atatürk; three continents, four seas:
I'm lost among reforms, reactions, sultans,
concubines, campaigns; an unfamiliar script—

but brought back home each time I find
a pencil mark in your familiar hand:
the date you closed your tired eyes
at every chapter's final line.

How much did you absorb, before
you reached the ramparts of Vienna, where,
as Suleiman forsakes his failed siege,
your annotations prematurely end?

Did The Ottomans change how you saw the world,
as its author clearly wished?
Could you still care how you saw a world
reduced, by then, to a square of sky?

And what of all these other works
arrayed from room to room:
five thousand books, at least, you'd read,
reread, recalled and quoted from?

I wish I'd asked, and now I can't:
which lines, ideas, protagonists
from this, now silent, store of words
most shaped the way you lived

your quiet carefulness, creating
method, manners, modesty from doubt;
how far that held your beast at bay;
if I should try to do the same.

Phil Vernon

Slicing Sourdough

I hold the golden loaf, tap the underside
with my thumb to hear the primitive drum.

Just as Dad taught me how to start
a cut with a crosscut saw with short

back-and-forth strokes, my first cut
with the breadknife consists of small

strokes to allow its serrated edge
to gain purchase in the hard crust,

before deeper cuts release the pungent
aroma of the porous, rough-textured inside.

I brush the crumbs from the cutting board
and lightly toast a slice. Butter melts

into the voids of the bread. And I recall,
with regret, that I failed to teach my son

to use simple tools: how to measure and mark
the cutting line with a square, how to begin

the cut and keep to the line for a true end,
how to start a nail with light hammer taps

before driving it home without bending the nail.

Too late now.

David Olsen

Bread and Butter

Wednesday is baking soda day.
The Saturday loaf is finished, and soup is on the horizon.
Wet mixes into dry, transmuting flour into dough.
Careful! It is prone to overworking – me too, babe!

The scent of baking follows me for an hour,
a friend to keep me company as I sing through work
that doesn't count as work: care and keeping.
Labour on labour.

I can hardly wait to turn it out,
tap for the hollow – though I must,
as steam rises like a memory of my grandmother's kitchen,
lest I burn my fingers like Gwïon Bach and suffer a goddess's wrath,
and all the knowledge of the world.

Lauren K. Nixon

DEFINED

It's suddenly there, in saddened, sobered eyes,
by thirty-five/forty, maybe even earlier,
or simply in the way a friend/foe walks –
a stoop, a wariness. No visible wound

but a sense of closing down, while deep inside,
where hopes of love and happiness once stirred,
or of wealth, success, a humdrum small voice hawks
its tiresome truths about how we're marooned

with any dream of 'making it' now over.
If all that's not enough, we're broken by
how time speeds up and no one can go back

to start again, or to switch to being another,
or to duck the daily question as to why

we're now defined by everything we lack.

Tom Vaughan

PAPER TRAIL

        Mother wasn't tall enough to cast a long shadow.
        Instead, she left a paper trail of handwritten notes
        in neat, well-rounded infant teacher's print.
        As if in sympathy with her young charges,
        she failed to master joined-up writing

Never precious about books, she used them
to mark family milestones and journeys.
In a book of nursery rhymes given to me
on my first day of school she inscribed
the date although it seems to have taken
several attempts to make it accurate.

        A weighty biography of Mary Queen of Scots
        begs *Please do not throw it away just*
        because I loved it and I hope you will too.
        The writing is scrawled, heavily underscored.
        The date, again corrected, March 26th, the day
        before she left the old house for a bungalow.

Thirty years of diaries starting with pocket ones
courtesy of the NUT are pensioned off with
generous week-to-view spaces in Dairy Diaries.
Notes on the back of envelopes are folded round
money for train fares, food or just to buy a coffee –
one still contains a £20 note (no longer legal tender).

        A journal of a trip to Capri is written on thick
        blue sheets of Basildon Bond. A note fastened
        with a safety-pin onto a striped cotton beach bag
        stuffed lumpily with my letters home begs
        PLEASE READ – ten years of your life are in here.

The most fragile inscription is the one she placed
under a white china figure on her dressing table.
In faded ink on foxed lined paper it reads,
Lady will you come with me
Over the dark, the wave tormented sea ...

No internet search has yet revealed the title of this poem.
I read it at her funeral and in the silence that followed
I seemed to hear a small voice whisper
Yes.

Ann Preston

The Dealer

9 APRIL 1946
(After Martin Figura)

Rain falls inexorably onto Axe Edge,
seeping through limestone cracks,
obstructed by stalagmites, it carves
a channel through Poole's Cavern, then
bursts from a rocky outcrop at Wye Head
to flow sedately through the Pavilion Gardens.

In town, a different kind of water,
warm and sulphurous, bubbling
with the expectation of miraculous cures,
attracts all the trappings of a spa resort,
crescent, pump room and thermal baths,
hydros and hospitals, hotels like palaces.

My mother is spreadeagled on a hard bed
in a small room lit only by a blue nightlight.
Her waters broke hours ago but the baby is breech,
facilities basic in the private nursing home.
Finally, Dr Clara Stewart decides her patient
has had enough and reaches for the forceps.

Two doors down the road, my father stokes the fire,
sits up all night in his sports jacket.
A week later, with his wife struggling behind,
he carries me home wrapped tightly
in a blanket. But I work both arms free
and waft them in the bracing Pennine air.

From my bedroom I could see The Old Hall
where Mary Queen of Scots was held under house arrest.
Allowed out to take the waters, she scratched a fond farewell
on her window. But hours spent gazing through
rain-streaked glass must have shown her the inexorable
approach of the day when the axe would fall.

Ann Preston

GHOST CHILD

and at the sound
of my voice
something stirred,
heavier than shadows,
in the next door rooms.

I stopped
and listened
as the voice continued,
a little deeper
more resonant
than my own,
but still familiar enough
to summon
the hushed shuffle
of tiny footfalls
and glimpse
this frail
shadow child
I've wanted to guard
and protect
over the years,
approaching my room.

no shiver
of recognition
in his unblinking
owl-large eyes
that stare right through me
as he sleepwalks
up and down
the unending corridors
and flights of stairs,
lost and trapped,
unable to hear
my guiding voice
calling out to him,
wandering in
unceasing circuits
through the many
spinning chambers
and echoing levels
within this house
of shadows.

Cosmo Goldsmith

SPIRIT GOOSE

After scrambling back down
from the cold, granite peak,
we gathered in the pop-up lodge.

The course convenor asked us
what we'd gained from the day,
his excitement grew

as we chose spirit animals.
My colleagues envisioned
the eagle, the lynx, the wolf.

I embodied the goose,
waddled round the fire pit.
I meant every honk.

Back at work, spreadsheets
on the screen couldn't be tallied
with the wilderness.

At lunch in the park,
a goose flopped by a bench,
too stuffed with bread to move.

I raised my arms,
and he raised his head.
to the bright silver sky.

He slipped into the lake,
then flapped and ran,
then flew into the North.

Back in the office,
I joined eagle, lynx, and wolf
as we stared at our screens.

Spirit goose,
I wish you well
on your journey north.
I hope to see
what you see:
the moonlit rivers,
the sunlit lakes.

Paul Bavister

SNOW GEESE

He looked as though he had done
time or done something for
which he should have done time,
but then he smiled.
He stopped me on the path
and asked what kind of birds
were on the lake. I said
I didn't know but guessed
snow geese, and he spoke
the words and glowed.

I continued to the lake
and found snow geese
by the thousands, droning,
rising, circling, settling
again, a sight like no other,
a sound like no other against
the boom of ice cracking
and the honking of what
I took to be swans.
I'm no expert in birds.

I walked back the way we both
had come, wondering whether
my meditations, too,
made me look jailable.

Jack Granath

Let Me Tell You a Story

about a river

where white-breasted dippers fly up
from the rushing weir
where elvers stroke stones
under coppered water
filled with the underside of sky.

Let me tell you a story about a river
and a woman who remembers

that girl with the gap tooth
frowning into her fringe
who ran into a sunny room
her arms full of roses
dropping them all to reach for a kiss.

Let me tell you a story about a path
along a river walked by a woman who is followed

by a robin
that stops and follows
stops and follows
and how the woman still dreams
the robin may be a dead man.

Let me tell you a story about a river path
that follows a railway track

and the station guard
with his frayed cuffs and collar
taking his time to pace along the platform
with its new asphalt and pansies
to unlatch the gate

who pulls back the oiled bolts
clanks down the signal lever
letting the tonnage of steaming metal
roll on, unobstructed
killing no-one.

Let me tell you a story about a river
and a woman and a railway track.

Let me tell you a story

Helen Scadding

WE SEE YOU, MR OWL

The children loved chopping up your pellets,
finding Lego pieces, Playmobil hands.
Always laughed at your impression of the coffee press.
Liked the way we used your beak for a peg
when we strung you on the washing line
to sleep off the night's excess.
Growing up, they watched you,
saw you as a God –
quartering fields, drop-hunting,
surprising them from TV antennas.

Then they learnt about the silent death you dealt in.
Tried to rebuild voles from the shards of bone
and lumps of fur you brought them.

One night, they caught you in mid-air,
held you, clasped between palms,
like a prayer,
they felt you.
Almost without body.
Hollow-boned, blinking stupidly,
singular, barbarous.

Tom Ratcliffe

PIGEON

Pigeons mimic my faults.
Overweight and wobbly
on their pins, they fight
like heavies in a bar
for croissant crumbs
on café deck planks;
corporations puffed-out,
bickering flutteringly.
Their shock droppings
mock your hair or shirt.

Massed cooing proclaims
co-ordinated take-overs
of urban space, not a cure
for human hearts that ache.

Once I fed a friend
in my downstairs room,
window open to let in
the balmy summer air.
A pigeon took its chance
between the iron bars
thieves bend with car jacks.
Panicking and shrieking
around the kitchen table,
it upset a wine bottle,
flapping too franticly
to find its way out.
My third grab cupped it
and out it vocalised;
a discombobulated diva.

Charles Lomas

WARBLERS
*(From the Guardian article: 'Palestinian birdwatchers
defy danger to scan the skies' – Marta Vidal 2024)*

That morning, a tiny brown warbler is caught
in the nets of an olive branch. It is brushed
and has its leg ringed with a rushed vow.

In Beit Jala, flocks of girls swing their braids
in sync to their steps. The golden and mouse-like
chiffchaff, claps its wings for them

and resumes its journey north.

Birds can travel wherever they want. The next morning,
as the nearby glocks click into place, a wanderer
keeps his promised eyes on the bleaching sky

but the Palestinian sunbird – its head foiled
and blue as a fish, the ashen body, and the persevering
wing-tips flashing like scales –

does not leave.

Connie Greig

ISRAELI LANDSCAPE
(After R. S. Thomas 'Welsh Landscape')
'In the new and horrifying post-October 7 reality, it seems that there is no longer room for empathy in Israeli society. That being the case, it is now time to expose the flip side of the coin: the terrible price we as Israelis pay to accommodate the policy of ruling over other people – because this is not just about the Palestinians; it is about us, too.' Alon Sahar, former IDF soldier.

To live in Israel is to try to forget
The spilled blood that ran
Into the making of each sunset,
Dyeing the immaculate Jordan
Draining into a Dead Sea.

It is to be unaware,
Beneath the roar of warplanes
And rumble of tracked vehicles,
Of strife in streets or grazing grounds,
Spinning with slings and gunshots.

There you can only live in the present,
Inventing past heroics
And a future paradise
Where Arabic is unspoken
Or at least unwritten.

There are cries in the dark at night
As sleepers are dragged from their beds,
An ambush of shadows in uniform,
Clatter of rifle butts and boots
Down stairs to camouflaged vehicles.

But the present is hollow
In the absence of a past
Brittle with the bones
Of mass graves under
The soil of bulldozed villages.

As ghosts rattle keys to their houses,
Knock to return to their tables,
A paranoid people
Infected with racism
Worries at the carcase of an old book.

Dave Wynne-Jones

After Seeing David Smith's 15 Medals for Dishonor *(antiwar art made from 1937-1940, in reaction to WWI)*

the curtain parts
the almighty hand of god reveals

the government armed
more deadly than the soldiers
a cannon straddles a woman
supine
the mind is raped
by every cutting implement
the press edited
lines laced with lies
a broadcasted repeat
radio frequency ablation

expunged
the vision blurs
smoke masks reality
communication bombs
the emotions, prostituted
the bodies, piled and burned
flesh falls
lungs blacken
death is nourished
children starve
the sky eats
the earth digests

a crimson tide rises
and runs north
hospitals sink
refugees drown
overcome by oppression
washed in fear
the law is spun dry
the pillars of justice are wound and held
around a finger
liberty hangs
by a noose

the occupiers take
remake and destroy
new coffins furrow the earth
revealing
history's skeletons
the wages of war are won
by machine makers

Annie Kocur

You Gallant Few

He spies his sash-window self, hoiks his tie,
hinges into the RAF Club, book-ended
by terraces with curtains in hessian-hues.
On its flagpole, the Spitfire Roundel chatters
at a cast-iron downpipe. Near the door,
back-street weeds and vermin boxes.

By 'Poppies for Sale', he signs the register,
taking in the linger of nicotine.
A bunch of daffodils droop, the seated
few who water their memories with sips
of stout. No clock hung up, ticking
to remind them not to go home.

Yesterday's Daily Mail curls in the bin
while pints are pulled to youth-of-today banter.
Careless talk only costs them the next round;
their gallivanting stayed by chronic pain.
Unfinished conversations slump about,
worn-out cushions on empty chairs.

The bartender, nods to him, then a poster:
'Wings Appeal – A Fundraiser Lunch Today'
A banner stuck across it blares out: Cancelled.
And some wit has scrawled: 'cos no one had booked.

Clifford Liles

Pinay Honey Ko

I'm back in Blighty in the winter cold,
The Philippines seems just a memory,
And there's no Pinay honey ko to hold.

It all seems magnified a hundredfold –
Past happiness and present misery.
I'm back in Blighty in the winter cold.

The days are dreary, too short and ice-cold.
The nights, alone, drag like eternity,
And there's no Pinay honey ko to hold.

Am I dreaming of those nights we rolled
Naked in bed together? I must be –
I'm back in Blighty in the winter cold.

There's nothing left: all that we had was sold.
I left my job, my friends deserted me,
And there's no Pinay honey ko to hold.

I dream again, seeking her unconsoled,
But when I come round to reality,
I'm back in Blighty in the winter cold,
And there's no Pinay honey ko to hold.

Christopher Webster

Note: Honey ko – a Filipino expression meaning 'my honey'

XENOPHOBIA

It was a moment the Earth had been anticipating for a millennium. The ship was detected long before it reached the solar system. The entire planet knew it was coming. There was no question. It was headed towards Earth.

Six months ago, it had appeared in the distant heavens and had been thought to be a comet or an asteroid. It had been duly labeled, then ignored.

Scientists at MIT had first discovered its unnatural trajectory. It was being navigated by intelligence. And it was headed towards the Earth.

World leaders convened summits and debated how to react to the arrival of the alien race. Scientists contemplated what new wonders were to be learned from a race capable of galaxy travel. Military leaders wondered how such a race could be defended against.

Theologians contemplated the effect the alien culture might have on the world's religions. Did the aliens even have a religion? Historians drew parallels with the arrival of Europeans in the Americas.

And still the ship drew closer.

Some thought it was the End of the World and gave themselves over to licentious abandon, as in every plague or calamity in human history. Junior High science clubs felt their wildest wet dreams of Star Trek and Star Wars were about to come true. The Guild of Science Fiction Authors called a conclave to discuss the myriad possibilities of First Contact. The event was well attended. The costumes alone made it a memorable affair.

There was a slight uptick in the suicide rate. But it could not be definitely attributed to the impending arrival of the aliens.

Like oceans drawn to the pull of the moon, people began to ascend mountains, setting up campsites where they painted signs of welcome and sang songs to the stars. Small pockets of worship grew up, with people worshipping the unknown race who hurled towards the planet. Even among these small groups, a schism arose; some sects broke free to worship the ship itself as a living entity.

And still the aliens drew closer.

On the third day of the seventh month of the modern calendar, the ship entered the Earth's atmosphere.

The vessel was nuclear powered.

The defense systems of the United States detected its atomic signature. The failsafe computer programs interpreted it as an attack from Russia. Because it was already well within U.S. airspace, emergency missile defense systems launched automatically, without human input. The Russian system detected the U.S. launch and released its own missiles. Other global systems, detecting these launches and detecting the atomic signature of the ship, launched attack and counterattack scenarios of their own – Pakistan against India, Israel against Saudi Arabia, Australia against China . . .

The entire offensive took less than three hours. When it was over, the Earth was a dead, burnt-out cinder. No life remained of any kind. No plant life. No insects. No bacteria. The waters were poisoned, the air burnt away. The Earth would never again be capable of sustaining life. It was almost a new star, emitting a strange, glowing light of its own.

The alien captain – not entirely humanoid, not entirely vegetable, semi-gaseous and partially liquid – used his light-sensory organs to stare at the plasma screen. He ordered warning buoys to be launched to inform other ships to stay away from the lifeless yet now deadly planet.

As the ship flew off toward another part of the galaxy, the captain contemplated. He had visited many worlds in many galaxies across the universe. Some were friendly, some hostile, some fearful, some bold. Some wanted to expand and interact, others just wanted to be left alone.

But in all his travels in all the worlds in all the systems he had explored, he had never encountered a race so xenophobic that it would cause its own extinction rather than say hello.

Mark Pearce

ISLAND

We scent our island on the wind:
grilled pollack, hottentot fig.
No matter how awful our daily lot
we can follow the swallows and guillemots,
voyage west where we belong,
breathe pure air, relax and live.

An ivied gatepost, carved celtic stone,
alive with bees and overgrown,
postbox, pub, village shop,
a gabled villa seen through mighty oaks,
the laughter of children we thought was lost,
few fences, nothing ever locked.

Thrushes rehearse their repertoire
on empty lanes that lead to the coast;
crystal waves break and unfold.
This place is etched on all our charts,
sings in our minds as things fall apart.
In recurring dreams we queue for a boat.

Martin Reed

THE GAUL

She was not a smack up from
Brixham or Plymouth
or Ramsgate to land catch in Hull
and go home
like The Bethel, The Dearing,
Elizabeth, Petrel
or Teaser, Teetotal or Thames. Or
even the Hull
built Precursor, Magneta or
Plover our grandfathers
and their fathers sailed. Nor later
the Beverley built
steam sidewinders: The Heron,
The Linnet
or Lark or The Goole, Thrush or
Auk. She was
The Gaul: 1106 gross tons, 216
feet, fillet-factory
stern-trawler, the latest,
unsinkable, through
the locks of St. Andrew's
dockside sailing
for Barents Sea north of Norway
with two crews,
one sailing and hauling, one
gutting and freezing
that January day. Thirty six out
from Hull and started
to fish, nets full for nine days,
with the Kelt and the Pict
and Swanella. Gaul damaged her
nets then put new
and by 23:30 7th February
reported all well. But by
02:00 the Pict and Kelt pulled
away gear, the winter
wrecking weather. Gaul reported,
"Laid and dodging."
The Mate on Swanella called
Gaul on the 8th; "Yer
a'right. We'll be under way
shortly. We'll get outta
y'road; we'll dodge more inta
land."
Gaul started to run before weather
and passed

Name	Role	Age
Raymond Atkinson	Factory Hand	33
Ronald Bowles	2nd Engineer	24
Clifford Briggs	Factory Hand	45
Sidney Broom	2nd Officer	28
John Chisholm	Junior Officer	34
Robert Chisholme	Mechanic	45
Paul Edward Clark	Spare Hand	31
Stanley Collier	Charge Hand	41
John E Doone	Radio off'cer	35
Brian Dudding	Spare Hand	23
James Gardner	4th Engineer	52
Eric Grundy	Factory Hand	42
Timothy R Hackett	Trainee Eng'r	22
John Heywood	Factory Hand	23
William E. Jones	Factory Hand	26
Terence Magee	Factory M'gr	38
James McLellan	Factory Hand	18
Colin Naulls	Spare Hand	32
Raymond Neilson	Factory Hand	41
Peter H. Nellist	Skipper	43
Thomas W. North	Factory Hand	26
James. W. O'Brien	Spare Hand	27
John R. O'Brien	Chief Eng'r	38

Dream Catcher 51

the Swanella a mile off starboard; 72.25 N, 25 E at 10:45. The Gaul's last echo showed her six miles astern. Since then the unsilence of sea and the comfortless emptiness left skylines and shorelines just promising hope. They said she'd've foundered, the winds storm force 10 with continuous snow. Impossible to see waves 50 foot high until they had hit. But we wondered, the spy ships— and why with no bodies, they'd not search. They refused and protested there was no such thing as spy ships. Though the Rairo reported nets snagged 72 N, 25 E in 75, they said it was too big a search area to search. It took 23 years, a small TV crew, to find there, the Gaul. Now 50 years gone, still they wait. Hope with mourning on.

Name	Role	Age
Neil Petersen	Cook	47
Joseph F. Riley	Spare Hand	52
Thomas Sheppard	Factory Hand	55
Clarence Smith	Plant Oper'tor	59
Maurice Spurgeon	Mate	38
Karl Straker	Ass'tant Cook	17
William Tracey	Spare Hand	24
James Wales	3rd Eng'r	29
David Wheater	2nd Cook	26
Harold Wilson	Spare Hand	27
Henry Wood	Factory Hand	56
James Woodhouse	Plant Oper'tor	47
Albert Worner	Factory Hand	45

Note: sometime on 8/9 February 1974, The Hull trawler Gaul disappeared without a Mayday. She was new but modifications were not entered into her records. The skipper, sailing her for the first time, was given out of date documents. She did not meet 4 of the 6 minimum stability requirements.

Angela Brodie

Song of the Alley

I don't know now and never knew
why the big ship sails down the alley-alley-o
on the first day of September
but it sails on, and on,
and Sally was always, oh,
the big-voiced pride of our alley,
the raucous thump of it
but you couldn't play marbles on cobbles
and nobody sings by the factory,
windows out and shreds blowing.

My love and I did meet
where the long-fingered willow
dips the green river,
weaving soft rushes
in the frame of the sky.
Now I cry *Oh Mr Wolf,*
may I cross your Golden River
and I can't quite remember
if it's the first day or the last.

Pamela Coren

SOMETHING OR NOTHING

Appearances of death can be proved false,
defibrillators can restore a pulse,
the leafless tree revives itself in Spring,
with each new dawn the birds wake up and sing.

Conductor-less, an orchestra will find
it takes a while to get themselves in time
so, it's too early to admit defeat
before our hearts have synchronised their beat.

A newborn baby often shuts its eyes
but there's no hurt because there's no surprise
and flowers always take some time to bloom
but nothing grows if it's not given room.

Elastic bands will stretch before they snap
and we recycle now before we scrap.
As magnets can attract or can repel,
to fall out means you liked me once as well.

The door is closed but only on the latch,
the perfect throw awaits the perfect catch,
like two ships sailing on a different tack
but not too late for you to call me back.

Chris Scriven

Fragments of Blue

On a day when she can feel the sharpness
on her shoulders, tiny claws digging into her skin,
when all she wants is to gouge them out
of herself, scream to the wind, she stands
in this room which she has stood in so many times before,
notices the sofa, sagging under the weight of memories,
achievements, arguments pushed down the sides of cushions,
hopes fallen down the back like tarnished coins
from a trouser pocket.

At the window she sees the blue which contains
all the birds of the earth, feathered flight trailing clouds
to become airborne boats, wakes mapping their course.
She sees a beetle on the window ledge,
the sun making a relic of its carapace,
inlaid with emerald and sapphire.

On the street she notices a child running,
legs seemingly too long for his body,
he uses them as springs, to leap and bound
after the bubbles his mother blows to the wind.
One rises upwards, escapes the boy's laughing hands,
floats towards her window, until she can see
its own tiny fragment of blue carried
on the inside.

Lisa Falshaw

The Art of Concealment

On Tuesdays I swallow my heart
like a bird reversing flight,
tucking love beneath my ribs
where it beats in secret code.
Some mornings I wake to find
my need has grown fur,
prowls the kitchen on velvet paws
while I pour coffee, pretending
not to notice how it winds
between his ankles, purring.
When the moon is full
I can let it show –
my wanting splits open
like a ripe fig, purple-sweet,
and I am permitted to feed him
pieces of my hunger
with trembling hands.
But most days I must fold
my yearning into origami shapes:
swan, boat, paper plane,
tuck them into drawers
beside the unmatched socks
and forgotten birthday cards.
At night, while he sleeps,
I count the ways I've hidden:
my love curled like smoke
in empty mason jars,
pressed flat between pages
of unread books, dissolved
in bathwater, transformed
into steam that fogs
the bathroom mirror.
Sometimes I wonder if he sees
how I've become a magician
of need, pulling scarves
of longing from my sleeves,
making desire disappear
behind my smile,
only to find it later
nested in my hair
like wayward sparrows,
building homes from things
I meant to keep concealed.

Louise Worthington

An Equal Music

I'm at the station, waiting for you to steer your way
through the crush that spills towards Glastonbury,

smells of dope, beer, oranges. You'll moan about the noise,
our lane being crowded with vans, but you'll leave water

by the garden wall for hikers. How impatient I am
for your solid profile, warm body, Renaissance hands

that can do anything, make anything, build the Sistine chapel
if they have to. I'm trying to read Vikram Seth,

but there's nothing that doesn't feed my hunger for you.
It's like wanting to pull someone out from under rubble,

to rediscover the shape of your shoulders, arms, embodied spirit,
though I know it's quite absurd – three decades, three blind mice,

since you'd meet me here. Anyway, what are you now, without
your body? And what am I, lost in this midsummer heat?

Rosie Jackson

MIRACLE

I expected fog without
the glow of service lights.
Sheet ice, not sunned tarmac.

I expected deadly silence
not your glorious song.
Sackcloth not soft skin.

The single line of your mouth,
not the warmth of your breath.
I expected an end

not the renewal of all things,
beyond the furthest reaches of our imaginations.
I expected resignation

not your open-ended love.

Andrew Senior

The Twilight Bus, the Last of Its Kind, Has Long Gone

& you say we'll walk back, chuckle
at my upturned canoe of a mouth

as we tackle the dunes. We've had a skinful.
Unhinged like first-step babies

across the weakling sand. Marram grass looking like
the worst case of bed hair you'll ever see.

It's darkening all the time. We are torchless
& that's what love should be like, you say. You're talking bollocks

to me, to the sika deer with binocular eyes
while naked figures flit between shore & sea,

unleashing their history before it grows coy.
You reckon passionate love

only lasts for twenty-seven months. Bodies
misplace their sexiness after fifty-two years. You keep diaries.

So at the foot of the pine line
where Studland Bay winks & nudges the naturist

we should strip, trick passion into thinking
it still has a hand in the game,

has legs that can run fast enough
to catch the last bus home.

Simon French

THE HEART-SHACKLES ARE NOT AS YOU THINK
(After a line in Mary Oliver 'When the Roses Speak, I pay attention' from Thirst, Beacon Press, 2006)

The heart-shackles are not as you think.

You are not imprisoned by authorities, pinioned
to a guard on the one and other hand,
enduring only to be hauled
before the judge.
No.
This heart
is a three-masted barque
rigged for roaring forties and far distant lands,
whose shackles will secure the wings billowing in every breath of wind.

Clare Bryden

Circle

HOUSEWORK

When I washed the walls of
junkyard stains you came
to me asking for water.
I told you to put down
your cane and let me wash
your hands instead, as if I had
some biblical claim
on your love. No, no, you said
and taking up the sponge
washed yesterday's bolognaise splash
from the night bright tiles.
I could have stepped in,
I see that now, steadied your hand
with mine and we could have
washed together in circles,
a kind of low-lit dance
polishing long after the stain
had gone.

When we held the teacups
at the memorial hall
we spilt each rain moment
like it was part of you. And as
I paused to shake each hand
at the doorway I felt your hand
in mine. All of us in the same
dance, cleaning the surfaces
we never paused to see.

Jet McDonald

Acts of Devotion

She was born the year Thatcher rose to power,
has never broken a bone, jealous of her sister's devil-
may-care ankle cast in plaster from tumbling

down banks. Bent over her studies
during the Falklands war, she was not allowed
to grow her hair. She needed that shy

silk curtain between her gap-toothed face
and the teacher she loved, whose high heels
clicked like abacus beads on the classroom tiles,

who gave her full marks but mistook her for a boy.
While Michael Buerk reported famine from Ethiopia,
she let it all go. In her wizened chest, her heart

rattled like a nut. On the empty ward,
she was sent a postcard of Mary of Bethany,
a rebel in ringlets with a book in her lap.

From the Bible at her bedside she read about her:
how she provoked her sister by kneeling
at the Teacher's feet; how Judas shamed

her extravagant devotion that filled the house
with its musky animal scent. Cried out,
If you had been here, I would not have died.

The year of Section 28, she returned
to pour nard over her teacher's feet,
wiping them dry with her long, long hair.

Elaine Ewart

This Won't Change Things

You came out on social media.
Not knowing how to respond,
she didn't text you for days,
though you knew she'd seen it.
You feared you'd lost her.
Looking back at your interactions,
did she see your relationship in a different light?
That time she rushed round with a bottle of red
at midnight when your husband left,
did you take her for a fool?
Yes, when you said her hair looked nice,
you meant,
You are the sun. Wondering at your luck,
that time you fixed her earring,
like a child releasing a rare crustacean
in a rock pool at low tide.
Yes, that time you rescued her from the cliff face
(that was not real and forms no part of her memories).
On Facebook her finger hovers over your queer status.
Why do you need to label yourself?
she pleads. As you turn away,
voracious under the restaurant chandeliers,
you're sorry to have taken her to this place
she doesn't understand.
She doesn't understand.
You're sorry to have taken her to this place.
Voracious under the restaurant chandeliers,
she pleads as you turn away.
Why do you need to label yourself?
On Facebook her finger hovers over your queer status
that was not real and forms no part of her memories.
Yes, that time you rescued her from the cliff face.
In a rock pool at low tide,
like a child releasing a rare crustacean,
that time you fixed her earring.
You are the sun, wondering at your luck.
You meant
yes, when you said her hair looked nice;
did you take her for a fool?
At midnight when your husband left,
that time she rushed round. With a bottle of red,
did she see your relationship in a different light?

Looking back at your interactions,
you feared you'd lost her.
Though you knew she'd seen it,
she didn't text you for days.
Not knowing how to respond,
you came out on social media.

Elaine Ewart

Les Goûts

'Straight' and 'queer'
are consumer brands;
two spiteful tribes,
with more in common
than identity politics
will let them let on.
Fascists obsess about
identity, so stick it
up your *Dasein*.
Lust mocks and shocks
us, so we all look silly.
Like Baron de Charlus,
we all have our *goûts*,
if not all quite like his,
but *prolé* Charlies lack
fancy life-choice menus.
For a *plat du jour* of love,
pop populism's Ps and Qs
keep you under the cosh.
Tight bands of libertines
or puritans snare frail prey
to paw or hound for a lark.
Sex brands rank on flesh;
Titania's rough trade with
Bottom sends Puck's sex
police to restore decorum.
If you just don't belong,
don't pretend you do,
cos nobody will believe
cringe-making fake you.
As Marx, Groucho not
Karl, never said, I'd
never join a club that
would have my member
as a member.

Charles Lomas

The Sound

this is the sound that silence makes
before the fall, before the break

before the night, before the storm
before this darker age was born

before the guns, before dissent
ripped us apart. Before the pent

up waters burst their banks and broke
homes and lives. Before the joke

history plays on all who hope
punch-lines deceiving horoscopes

before the body is discovered
before the moment when two lovers

cannot find the words which once
promised faithful permanence

this is the sound before the crowd
panics, and runs. Before the loud

speakers wake the prisoners.
Before the executioner

pulls the lever and you drop
to where both sound and silence stop

Tom Vaughan

THE LIGHT SWITCH MOMENT

'How do they do that?' I would say,
'I mean really: How do they do that?'
These people in joggers or shorts,
wooly hats and earphones in,
smart watch and faces set.
One track.
'How do they do that?'

Sometimes I would try,
after a few strides the strain would rise,
and the motivation fade,
and I'd stop.
The incredulity remained.

I tried again,
and again,
and came back the refrain:
'How do they do that?'

I didn't notice that the strides got imperceptibly longer,
and the distance imperceptibly further,
and one day, out of nowhere,
suddenly, surprisingly, and quite like magic:
A light went on!

I went past the pontoon where the swans and black-headed gulls gather for food.
I went past the ancient, gnarled oak tree, where it stands on the bend of the river.
I went beyond that bend, where the path turns away from the water's edge.
I went nearly to the end of the first football pitch,
for suddenly, amazingly, I could run!
And since then, I have run and run and run!

Cathryn M. Spiller

The Ruins of Lowestwood Mill, No Soundtrack

She spots her after filming soft sunlight
on the sensuous curves of corrugated iron –

a woman in pink with slow draw cig,
still as a lizard – bleach blonde,
skin like packet pastry, derailed,
who leans out of the glassless window
of the scuttled weaving mill.

Though she can only see her top half,
she knows her legs are thin as laths,
that she has blisters from harsh heels,
that she is grey-tired as well as young –

the wounds men have scarred her with
have turned to beaked things that flap
against her pointy ribs.
  It's her turn
to be lookout – flesh business lurks
behind her in the dank shadows –
hurried, cash in hand moistness.

She scowls through the film-maker,
frowns her away. No choice

but to walk off, hold this stark memory
that will always accompany the soft light –

how she'd like to film the woman
as a tall reed with a steep field
in the background, calmly waving
or sitting by the packhorse bridge,
humming a tune she's always loved
while she dangles her callused feet
in the frayed hem of the river.

Adam Strickson

STAINED

Here's Mary, gazing up. Afraid.
An angel reaching down.

Her ultramarine robes, her halo;
Gabriel's buttercup hands
offering comfort to a country girl
in the family way.

I'd pay real money to hear
the words he said to Joseph
when he tried to walk out on her.

Lauren K. Nixon

SELF PORTRAIT

there's a face in the mirror   it's mine   I'm drawing it   3B pencil moving fast   keeping contact with the paper swiftswift   soft look   drawing feels like loving   4B 5B 6B so soft   there's a question I'm evading so effectively I don't even know what it is my wrist hurts   forget the background   forget the hair   no rubbing-out   I like how my face is cracking like August earth is tender   I haven't wanted to look at myself lately   but something   *she*   wants to make herself known   7B 8B 9B softsosoftsosoftso   seeking more of a likeness than a likeness   dot delicate the inside corner of my eye which is and always seems to be   the starting place   skate the white page   swift to edge of nose   skim to mouth corner   hover on a breath   dart eastwards to earlobe   scurry small circles   no longing now to separate surface and tip   touch my crease cluster half-face blossoming   from the centre to magnetic space   draw back to eye   wing sudden   sweep the socket high from outer lash through lines which might be data   up through years of brow fly my father's forehead folded in my own   put this here where ugly is   and today we will do without our hair

Rachel Goodman

Another Self Portrait

She's in Rome, Florence, Venice,
Delft in Holland's Golden Age,
Paris, London, New York,
Germany between the wars.

She wears wimple, crinoline,
widow's cap, national costume,
paint splattered dress,
nothing but an amber necklace.

She's probably a man's possession,
wife, chattel, pawn, dependent, ward
and, or, mother, carer, nurse, muse.

She's dreaming, working, studying,
advised, abused, patronized, ignored,
possibly tutored by father, brother
or trusted family friend.

She's poor, cold, hungry, barred, bored,
crippled with pain, just not strong,
ripe with vibrancy and life,
destined to die young.

She's not in life room, atelier, academy
till time passes, very rarely in gallery,
seldom ever in history books.

But alone in front of her easel
with pigments, palette, brush,
her eyes looking into the mirror,
she shows herself to us.

Andria Jane Cooke

Nude Models

Two days a week I left my high school English class – Don Quixote and Dulcinea, Catharine and Heathcliff, and Miss Elliot, on whom I had a crush – a little early to drive to Kenyon College for figure drawing. This was my first encounter drawing the nude human form. Well, almost. Terri, a girl I was hoping to date, agreed to pose for a single session and a single drawing, reclining in a black vinyl bean bag chair in the corner of my room. Within a few minutes of scribing the page, my regard of her switched from the romantic to the analytic and aesthetic. I was in love with her, but I was more smitten with the comprehension of how to depict the female form – the desire to make an excellent drawing.

The figure drawing class was held on the upper floor of Bexley Hall, an odd, red brick gothic revival building. The students, all about a year older than me, sat on drawing "horses," simple bench-like furniture where we leaned our drawing boards and with pencils, conte and charcoal painstakingly replicated a model's pose on identical sheets of paper. It was an exciting time as I gained a sense of what art school might be like. The models, young, thin, work-study students, were adequate, but the poses were rarely challenging. At the outset of one session, when the usual model didn't show up, the instructor asked another art student, a veteran of the class, to pose. With no hesitation, he stripped down and took his place. I found this more unsettling than when a model arrived for the pose in a robe. The act of disrobing made him more naked than nude. The models were often situated in a chair on top of a table. One painfully shy girl, on her first day, was so seated and after a drawing or two I noticed that her chair had shifted so that one chair leg was hanging off the edge. I could see the impending disaster but froze because if I called her attention to her peril, she would likely fall. And I was too shy to approach her. When the professor came my way, I would say something to him. But she shifted and both model and chair flipped over and off the table. Somehow, she landed on her feet. Though shaken and embarrassed, she was unharmed, but no longer keen on modelling.

The next fall, at art school, I mounted my drawing horse every Monday morning after art history, just like fourteen other eager 18-year-olds in tie-dye and ratty bell bottom uniforms. We came to know the bodies of a variety of models, and they became part of our routine. They could be seen in their robes, smoking in the hall, or getting a cup of coffee or soup from the vending machines. We all groaned inwardly and rolled our eyes at one another when Perfect Girl was the model of the day. She was beautiful. Blonde, pale, petite and flawless. For the first ten minutes of our first class, most of the boys were in love with her and the girls were embarrassed for her – for the necessity of her nakedness. But soon we discovered her perfection was impossible to draw. It was as if our pencils refused to latch onto her contours. She was like drawing mist. Equally difficult was Yoga Guy. He had a long thick beard and graying hair that extended to his waist. His poses were extraordinary and daring in flexibility, often striking headstands and other ridiculous yoga positions. However, he was so skinny that if you happened to get a side view of his pose he nearly disappeared. The results on the page were what looked like hairy sticks. And then there was The Adonis. When he shed his robe, the women in the class became particularly quiet, but everyone was in love with him. Athletic, tastefully muscular, exquisitely proportioned, his poses were dynamic and inspiring. Our drawings were exquisite on Adonis days. In sculpture class we modeled clay figurines of Curvaceous Mom. At forty-something, her body and the way she carried herself projected the confidence of a mother. For boys a long way from home, we wanted her to wrap us up in her arms (clothed of course) and tell us everything would be just fine, that we would be brilliant artists – and maybe take us home for dinner.

There were a couple of oddballs. The Exhibitionist (aka, Happy-to-See-You-Guy) was a strangely shaped, squat, balding man. The male models usually wore a typical athletic supporter purchased in a sporting goods store. This guy donned a size-too-small black leather apparel obtained from an entirely different venue. Walking past the drawing studio one morning, I caught a glimpse of him posing for another class. He flashed a creepy smile while an obvious erection strained at his inadequate covering. For painting class Bathing Beauty was integrated within an enormous and complex still-life construction in the center of the room. She couldn't seem to sit still, the only skill required, and after an hour or so of fidgeting, lost interest in the task, wandered over to the paint encrusted sink and began splashing water on her body, rubbing her limbs and humming, seemingly heedless of her incredulous onlookers. Her new preferred pose reminded me of a Greek Venus we studied in art history. The students felt sorry for her and after a bit, the professor gently shepherded her from the room.

Years later, as a new professor, for the first figure drawing class I taught, our model Tracy was pregnant with her first child. We were all her family on Tuesdays and Thursdays as we watched her belly, breasts and ankles swell over the course of the semester, her progress charted in the students' drawings. We threw a little shower for her, and her baby arrived a week after the final critique.

David Sapp

South Facing

Sunlight's the problem, you insist.
It quarries colour from furniture, fabric,
our Van Gogh sunflowers.
We must starve it of fodder, snap
on the handcuffs. Grey is not an absence.
It's a quiet boiling.

Now, there's no smack-me-yellow
muslin drapery, no
hot tomato two-way love seat, no
lightning gold in our Berber weave, no
pot pouri of deep pea-green
to float us away.

Now, we're gravel, asphalt,
storm-cloud, lunar landscape, sterile
inside a rabid purity
that makes me want to scream out:
PINK! VERMILLION!! TYRIAN PURPLE!!!
and Jackson Pollock them at the walls.

Claire Booker

AUTOMAT
(After Edward Hopper 1927)

Forgive the intrusion but I can see
you too are familiar with the night.
No-one calls you home; you sit alone
in the built absence of *Automat*.

I am drawn to your porcelain face,
that un-gloved hand I imagine
will tremble as you lift
the warmed cup to your lips.

I too have felt the city's critique,
the cold comfort of solitude.
You remind me I am not alone,
a brief anchor in a tranquil place.

I have studied you closely,
though I cannot guess your regret
or suppose our separate lives
are bound by a mirrored light.

I have no part in your film noir.
There is no shared denouement,
despite the lure of painted lips,
or an afterthought of red apples.

John Scarborough

But I Diverge – A Ghazal

It might seem that I tread quite different ground to you,
or maybe that I'm acting tightly wound to you.

I say I need more time in solitary muse –
nevertheless I find I'm tightly bound to you.

I'm self-conscious in social situations –
I need you, that's why I keep turning round to you.

I guarantee that I'm the most intense of friends –
I'm always acting as a faithful hound to you.

I make a joke of things I don't find humorous –
it's easier to try to be a clown to you.

The made-up music that I sing around the house
is senseless jabber, just a jangling sound to you.

My fixations are boundless – I can't tell you all
the information I'd like to expound to you.

My brain throws out connections, a spectrum of light –
mere quirkiness that's worth less than a pound to you.

People like me were tried as witches in the past –
that's why I'll always be hospital-gowned to you.

When life has burned me out, I cannot reignite –
it's like I'm lying in my burial mound to you.

It's hard to name it in a way you'll understand –
neurodivergence is a foreign town to you.

As starlings gather to make patterns in the sky,
my true experience is out of bounds to you.

Clare Starling

SHADOW BEES

After years of feeling she never fitted in
that her family just fussed around
and never understood her darkness

she dreamt bees swarmed at her window
and she welcomed them in and woke
without a single sting.

The next week she had a thrumming
box of bees on the back seat of her car –
her family watched from the house

as she coaxed the queen
into the warm pine of the new hive
and when workers flew into sunlight

her family cringed. She was positive
and for months looked forward
to warm honey dripped on toast.

The bees ignored the bright meadows
and found orchids and creepers
that rarely bloomed on the hill's dark side

and the unrecorded black bell flower
to make a botanist faint if ever discovered
in the overgrown valley.

Those bees worked hard to collect
half frozen nectar and powder themselves
with chilled pollen. As Autumn closed in

she tested the honey and shivered
and when she handed round the spoon
her family looked at her with surprise

having tasted the landscape's darkest shadows.

Paul Bavister

MOURNING THE QUEEN
'But for all their courage, bees know the worst of life' (Virgil, The Georgics Bk. IV)

I heard the humming first indoors –
hovering by next door's eaves a huge dark cluster
shifts to the ventilation grid, in seconds
smoothly flows through to their new home.
Outside only the guard bees' mesmerising rise and fall.

My first wild hope – no-one had seen but us.

Rain sent them in, sun drew them out,
our ears filled with whirring wings.
Three glorious days we shared their watch,
shadowed by apprehension – I wish
I could have warned the queen.

He could have been a bee-keeper
climbing the ladder, swathed with
veil round broad-brimmed hat.

My second wild hope – he'd save them yet.

He sealed the grid, cut off all escape,
only the guard bees stranded without,
their queen and colony entombed within.
All that long day, denied their queen
they rose and fell, stuttered, rose and fell.

I wanted not to look, shared their distress
till one by one they stalled and dropped to earth.
All gone next day, and still
the sealed grid drew my grieving eyes.

I'm trying to forgive my neighbour,
know others would have probably done the same.
My last vain hope – what might have been
if only the queen had graced our house instead.

Heather Deckner

Time on the Doorstep

It's a fine threshold –
the best we've had –
sufficiently old;
the steps are cracked,
high as a lost temple's

if the pond were a jungle mere.

It's a full front – intact:
just three strides
to neighbour and to gate.
There are clematis, climbing rose,
alpines and crocuses
and each time I come here,
usually from making
tetchy red remarks to students
or tidying minutes,
I resolve to stand more often
marking time on the doorstep.

It's spring now,
spattered with blue squill,
balmy. The steps rise
shedding dry husks
of winter hours
that withered here
one by one. I poke out
of an evening and intend
in summer to slouch
or perch here,
knees raised – a still dance
in time to welcome.

I'll have hanging baskets, too,
a pot of strawberries
and sweet yellow tomatoes
all within reach.

Or maybe I'll crouch
where leaves
feathery seeds and bents
collect in the corner

under the milk bottles
and reflect how I didn't –
and that will be good too
so long as there's more
time on the doorstep

and you'll be coming through.

Richard Smith

PLANTED

If they planted me in Autumn, under damp clods
tamped down with thick-soled boots,
and I waited through pillow-close nights,
when beetles and worms burrowed closer,
used my suffocated breath to heat their bodies,
if I stayed underground, seen only by the chill gaze of the moon,
would I now be pushing up towards the sun?
Would blossom unfurl in my eyes?
Would seeds spill from the dark cave of my mouth?
Would swallows nest in feather-down hollows in my cheeks?

Would you look for me in the Spring?

Lisa Falshaw

Everyday
After Yu Xiuhua

I've tried hard at life: to earn the right
to sink into the ground. I love

between   the cracks
of routine, live with the uncertainty of you, sit

in darkness
not counting the cost of breathing.

Mornings I drink tea, have a shower between cups
I take an interest, try to keep informed, look

between the pages, underneath the lines

then

lying in bed, I hold your memory close
like a photo in a wallet

fall

into a deep well
wake up, with tears in my throat.

Marius Grose

ASH

That strange habit you had
comparing people to trees

your best friend birch for all her grace
rowan so easily your elegant mother

willow your weak-willed father of course
and aspen for that ever-nervous uncle

you chose oak for yourself
which needed no explanation

all that strength and knowing beauty
so steadfast and self-assured

but I could never understand
why I'd been given ash

until years after we parted:
I discovered its brittleness

the readiness to snap
the willingness to be burned.

Shaun Barr

Déjà Vu

Here, the silver pin
through which I drain

away. I feel no less
than who I was

and yet an eighth
that all my heart

could hold is in a plastic
bag, rocked slowly

back and forth.
Does it sense me

like a missing limb,
or does it sleep,

till poured into
another's veins,

to wake with dreams
of who it used to be?

Andrew Pearson

The Man in the Clock

There's a silhouette-man in a giant clock
suspended over the Friday rush
of Praed Street crowds scurrying for trains;
his legs point at twenty-five to five,
like an alternative set of hands.

It's not some novel promotional gimmick
as I first thought, no hologram,
animated James Bond figure;
this isn't Leicester Square after all.
He's real up there, sealed behind
the ivory face, the black Latin numerals
and, though he suggests a presiding God
of infinite Time, he's merely cleaning.

Now the shadow-man in his circular drum
is trapped as a troubling memory,
a jester ignored by frenetic crowds
as he morphs into something rodent-like
in an exercise wheel, racing to nowhere,
mimicking the self-driven crowd
in earnest pursuit of their own importance,
contentment forever out of reach
as the hours lumber on, circling the dial.

Martin Reed

JENGA

He's the wrong actor for the part of sleeping rough – office hands, clean fingernails, the startled look of that famous Afghan girl, in the National Geographic. We find him perched on a bench, a small rucksack, a new red sleeping bag, in a churchyard, in the centre of Nottingham. He clutches the bag to his chest, gazes up as people hurry past, his cap empty, except some coppers and a 50p. I've only credit cards, but you find a £2 piece in the lining of your coat.

Like that dog, dumped from a large blue Jag, at the intersection by your house, which waited, all night, beside the highway, ears pricked at every braking car, which whined and trembled at a bagel tossed from a window, his eyes brim, as hand to heart, he bows his head, mouths silent thanks.

As much from the guilt of fortune, as charity, I go back later, with £20 from a cash machine. I had not expected tears, or a voice modulated to the corridors of Eton. I sit down beside him.

His name is Robert. He has no family, no friends, doesn't know where he'll sleep, where to find a meal, where to wash, or where to charge his I-phone. No-one has spoken to him since dawn, the sun now teetering on the rooftops, in a clear November sky. I listen, because I'm afraid of his pain. I don't ask him where he lived, what he did, if he grew up somewhere close by, how old he is. I don't ask him where it all went wrong. When I rise I shake him by the hand. As I walk away, I pause beside the gate. We stare, his face buried in shadow. I turn and walk away.

Andrew Pearson

TWO DRUNKS, ONE PARK BENCH, NEW YORK CITY, 1984

'e sez if ya get duh first punchin
yer sure ta win

well i dunno bout dat
baaah if ez drunk an' on duh floor
den mebbe

yeah, if ez drunk

deez daze
i tell ya
itsnot like duh ol' daze, duh sixies?
back den everyting waz diffrent
y'cud go where ya wanna
sleep where ya wanna

den der waz dem mooments
wimen an' blacks
wantin' respeck
dey got nuttin' frum dat

nah. dey din't neether

deez daze
jeeeeez
a guy can't e'en wok 'roun duh ciddy drunk n'more

Annie Kocur

Coffee and Cigarettes

ÉTUDE 60

anywhere, to alight anywhere will do,
end up in a library, turning the pages,
lost as ever, once the bus stopped:
there's no 9 to 5 of the soul, no clock
to tell you who you are, why you're there,
you're a number of days, to be ticked off,
dated and filed away: you were noticed, perhaps,
by a beggar come in from the cold, to rest
in the reading room, raising his head,
a fellow, say, of infinite origin,
sharing the air a while, and the miles behind him:
here's stillness, the hush of an other body,
the same bodies out there, barely brushing,
same entering of an elsewhere, the endless coming,
and infinite going: the same, between the pages
before your eyes, the ciphers of some precedent,
a poem, say, a piece of news, the field of print
and feel of the paper, touch of warmth when needed:
my need, and the beggar's, who seems to be sleeping,
met for a while, after 5, in the tumult of so much quiet

Ray Malone

Normal for Selby

He's quiet for a giant. As he lurches past, his bare head is level with my barer bedroom window. The house is modest but he'd dwarf the Dinka and all that meat should make some noise. There's none from him and none from me, like we're shoaling through a pattern of play, two scholarship ballers. He's oblivious though, as my Sudanese opponents never were, cornering the courts of Oakland, smiles as sharp as their elbows.

'Warriors,' I say to myself.

Mine's no frat dorm now, less animal than mineral house, narrow like a cleft in rock, like a coffin. Narrow house being another name for a casket in the before. We don't corner much world once we're flat-packed. I'm dreaming the coffins in courses across Doggerland because you can't bury half a billion Europeans. Dreaming the bike ride beyond Hull to that final wall. Dreaming when I should be tracking the giant down the approach road.

Out into the grey light I've grown used to, as I had the fog off the Bay or the smoke from the wildfires, I figure-eight round to him via the swan's road of the old canal then the wooden bridge. There's an earthwork that allows me to be eye-level or close when I don't hesitate, when I hail him. 'Now then!'

The giant doesn't answer though does halt mid-lane as I seem to arrive as he leaves. Brings his left paw to his hairless head and blinks.

'I'm Erickson,' I say.

He nods.

'How's the walking?' I try. His loose garb hinders diagnosis but I think the giant's favouring his right side. Doubt I could stretch his frame, despite having become a physio after being canned by Berkeley, because game night or no we'd been out tailgating when not in the frat. *Party like it's 1999* could've been our motto. Except that twenty-first century summer, a million acres of California went up in smoke. The ashen fear stretched from carpark to stratosphere.

'Rafel mahee amek zabi almi,' the giant says.

How were our littluns not terrified of us? His words seem inside me. *Fie!*

'I'm going the way you're coming,' I say.

He shakes his head, 'Always here.'

What? You wait years for a conversation and then this. I'm hazy on how long it's been. Selby was post-apocalypse even pre-, factories on his scale, with brewing and baking and other tors of industry ready to topple either side of Gowthorpe, further down which road I resided undisturbed, until today. It's the kind of place I could've afforded in the before, when up the A19 is one fork for the Archbishop's Palace or another for a penthouse by the Ouse. The river isn't really drained, nor the North Sea it feeds, though the water has receded, is corpsey beneath that glaze of algae, not moving, as the air above does not much move, as there is the stillness of meat on a hook to him.

'Always,' he nods.

'I'm from Thule, originally.' Home to outliers, where my brief summer returns saw hornets as unlikely as flying thumbs. 'Were your family here?'

'Family?'

As if he's fatherless. 'The ones like us.'

In two calipering strides the giant leaves the blacktop, palms me like a pet, and returns to the road. From one of us there's an animal stink. Though I swear I hear wolves when there's a rare wind, the other mammals are gone, the insects too, and the good birds, the ones who never learned to raid bins, went hungry to the trees then fell in flocks like autumn leaves.

'None like me,' he says.

NfS, I think, which was what doctors wrote when patients attended with their first tail, their second head, their third eye. *Normal for Selby*. Doctors from York, I mean, all of thirteen miles away. There was a Normal for Stoke too. A Normal for Norwich. A different flocking. Them and us, camps and walls, even then.

Dragging his foot across the tarmac through the blood - is that mine? - the giant stands me on the other side of this red line. I'm reminded of the blackbirds in Oakland, same marking on their shoulders, different species to ours. He raises his great head to inhale. There's a lake of byproducts nearby, an imperishable tarry sludge, but belly-filling. He can smell it, or me. My nosebleed. *Fi!*

'Good eating,' the giant says.

You wait years and I'd swap every word we'd said to hear one blackbird sing. Either species. I follow as he lurches off-road, crashes through the factory wall, and enters my lake. The giant drinks the syrup as the blue whales in the Bay come spring once would have krill. The world was so full! Isn't he leaving, or am I to make him? His leaving might restore the unmarked roads of an unmarked home. The dreaming, that is.

As my lake is off-limits, I eat outside town, mainly popcorn from the multiplex. I warm the poppers then sow the grain. A handful of kernels soon corners a room and an armful of memories sink me. That carny smell that coated stadia and date-nights. Timeless as our frat motto. Nor does the oil go off or the salt or the corn. I read of a Judean date palm seed that sprouted after millennia. One-third of the world's grain varieties were archived in Thule to re-green us. But there is no us, nor the syrupy yellow bandwidth of light to kindle and carry the fire of photosynthesis.

'The last one is a slow one,' I say.

It takes weeks to charge the solar capacitors I rigged to power the poppers, which physics and engineering and food science I learnt from library books. Learnt to fix my bike too. Might've learnt - if the stratosphere was safe again; if the aviation fuel, unlike the oil, was stable - learnt to reach the homeland. But there's nothing there now, as was said of

Canada. *Cà nada*. NfS, you know? I don't miss them, the flock, used to zig when they zagged in their surge for murmuration. Which *was* a marvel - at one remove. Whereas from within, aping every breakneck turn just seemed to me unfree.

The thing is, all the befores fade. I recall little prior to the giant's arrival. After, the factories have been swept aside like crumbs from his tablecloth. With lakeside clear, he advances on town, levelling the buildings like a bored JCB. In the structures still standing the giant leaves his excrement, every day a different midden, and wipes his ham-hock arse on library stock. There'll be no new books. Nor learning of any kind. I won't know why the world is empty, algal, greyer than medieval glass. I myself make nothing new. Being alone isn't enough to. But being together isn't enough to save him. He is a shitter and a despoiler, like ruins are a relief.

I scramble over the brick scree to his den. The giant's in my lake and I offer him the flag I brought from the Abbey, which is levelling very well without him. Perhaps he's just an accelerant? Doesn't know any better, as he's never been taught to remove his clothes before wading. I ask again, 'Is there anyone else?'

He looks down and down at me and my flag. 'Else like you?'

I mean, it's a towel if those are clothes. I'm willing him to do or say one interesting thing.

'No littluns since me kin,' he continues.

'Where are they?'

'Grew me teeths.' The giant lowers his head, grunts. 'Good eating!'

'Sorry?'

'Miss that fresh,' he shrugs at the syrup.

'So why are you still here?'

'Not hungry now.'

Fo! It's only a matter of time if I continue to corner him. I leave the towel behind.

It's doubtful my lake could be poisoned even if it wasn't essential. He's doubtless my superior, physically. I get reading again. They don't live long, not Giant Bradley nor Byrne the Irishman nor Öndör Gongor. Still, I've no wish to outwait him. I try *The SAS Survival Handbook*, *The Odyssey* and *Beowulf*. But it's the Book of Samuel that reminds me I'm being dim. Absent the flock, the human spark gets banked, year on year. I just need a gun for Goliath. A shotgun, really, for its range point blank.

There are many possible arsenals hereabouts, which farmhouses I'd previously stripped of pickles and preserves. Beyond those, in the before it was carrots and potatoes, disgorged in great dirty heaps from the Humberhead levels and onto the backs of lorries that would bounce open-topped to tables. The Dinka reckoned their wealth in cattle. Now I'll kill for syrup. Or so I say. A *towel?*

I'm days into the search, biking the spans between homesteads, then locking up and bouldering the ruts that were once approach roads.

Arriving at Forest Farm, I catch myself in a deep breath as I edge through the door and enter the airless kitchen. It's in sticky disarray. Rooms tend to be, their corners no longer cornered. When the mains power stopped and the sirens started, the flock didn't shelter in place this time, didn't even stop to pack. Headed for the high ground. Headed inland surely. Headed south. Their gun cabinets remained. Nothing mounted here, mind. As I open the under-stairs cupboard a footy bounces out across the catching tiles. Astonished that it's still inflated, I palm it. Little smaller than a basketball.

The light went long in Oakland and even on courts without floods we'd be balling into the dusk. Not tired, never tired, but barely able to see the rock. Which didn't matter because it came to hand, to mine and theirs, boys from farms and former conflict zones and future. When my Dinka roomies got up on tiptoes to war, went first home then to The Hague, that was my first breath in the after.

I'm still clutching the ball when I see the gun cabinet inside the cupboard, and the key inside the key cabinet. Not easily disarrayed, farmers.

I lay my ambush in the library, to which he'll return for a re-up, as if that excuses it. Then there are hours and days but it is a balm to be around books.

When the giant finally trails his own shit in, like a slack-bowelled lead goose, there's a farmyard stench. Is that why I'm struggling for air? I certainly can't spare any to speak as I rise on jelly knees to fire the Supreme de Luxe. The recoil from the first barrel surprises me and I pull the shot. Not a warrior. Instead of striking centre mass, I unstitch his right arm at the shoulder.

I see only that beading, and hear nothing, clearly not him spitting back song like a startled blackbird. I loose the second barrel. It finds that jointing again, removing his right arm. The giant looks down and down, as if sad the meat will go to waste, then follows his limb to the floor. *Fum!* Only radiating red lines to despoil the books now and, from my nose, more blood to flock with his.

Once the last spark is out, however, I have no appetite for my lake. Instead it'll be delicious to be done.

Yet I sit with his burst body till dark before cycling down the A63. I'm looking for a lit junction, whiting LEDs and night-green flora and signs for turns - how the heart would lift!

Finding no such oasis come the fog of morning, I lock up my bike to a lamppost and lay down in the road. I'm remembering the clearer air of Oakland my sophomore summer. Alone, my roomies gone from games, I'd uncorner on the carpet. Contra the steel of home, the light of SoCal made me feel honeycombed, sweetly in-between. I think dying will be like going to sleep while it's still daytime. There's no trick to it if you're tired, and I am.

Greg Forshaw

The Luthier's Gift

No fiddle yearns like the viola.
No other instrument aches
in a minor key like that,
like an old-school film star –
not too loud, landing perfectly
on the top of a phrase when
you thought she might not make it,
the migrant of the orchestra
with her own mysterious clef,
aloof in a foreign language
which we don't understand
so just smile, affect empathy
and wallow in that sonorous lament,
poured from the varnished maple soul –
and when you well up,
cry softly.

Jane Newberry

Now the Church is in a Blaze

In the bleakest part of the night, with candle lanterns,
they made their way down the hill – Evan Jones
of The Swan, old Bevan who loads his rattling bones
into the back pew, Bethan the Dairy who turns
to greet the curate, Will of the Red Farm.
They've come to sing the plygain, cock crow carols
that tell the Saviour's story, from Herod's peril
to scarlet Pilate, thorns and resurrection's calm.

They cram the firefly aisles, sing and sing
the long carols till hunger bites and they see
the sun at first light, born in a baby
for whom bronze bells will ring and ring.
Centuries later, I drive to that valley of plygain
because danger is close. I need to believe again.

Adam Strickson

Note: Plygain is a traditional Welsh Christmas service, which takes place between the early morning hours of darkness and sunrise on Christmas morning.

Polymorphous Perversity Bach

If all infantile happiness
is polymorphous perversity,
I'm four, dancing barefoot
on a thick, stringy, worn rug
to Bach preludes and fugues
played on a resonant piano
whose sound resounds from
the fake wood, spindly-legged
Stereogram in the far corner
of a book-cluttered lounge,
oblivious to which orifice
the pleasure comes through.
I've never been happier since.

Charles Lomas

MORENDO

On the window an ice frond
sublimes in weak winter light.
The smell of stagnant air.
A dusty piano is imperious
with the authority of a diva
whose gaze conveys reproach
for inattention. Beneath
a padded seat, the bench conceals
failed ambition: Hanon exercises;
major and minor scales;
sonatas and bagatelles;
preludes, waltzes, etudes.
Not even *Für Elise*, composed
for a child, was mastered here.
Awaiting clearance agents,
the inanimate room is silent.

David Olsen

Note: Morendo is a musical term meaning dying away.

FOLK IN TUNE

Thank you for attending.
This is our last song.
It's always been a favourite.
Please don't sing along.

We know this is a Folk gig.
You want to all join in
but judging by the evidence,
none of you can sing.

Your pitching is impeccable.
Your phrasing, just sublime.
Your diction is quite wonderful.
Your handclaps, bang in time.

You need to sing much flatter.
Start mumbling your words.
As Folk singers, you really are
the worst we've ever heard.

Simon Tindale

Audience to Comic

Say what can't be said
make light of things
make dark of things
in the private ear
in the public hall.
Be poor among rich
stir up the centre
eavesdrop on our deafness.

Bring gesture,
bring your bladder on a stick,
your horny forked nature.
Bring your honey speech
and your thistle speech.

Be a jerk, joke the jakes.
Take us out of the cage.
Drop off the crag, carrion crow,
bring us juice of the word.

Gag on our stuffing, jongleur.
Smack the flat of our tin swords
on your joker's anvil.

As for us, we'll sit in rows,
squirm the rusty spigot open
and from the deepest pit of all
we'll let the laugh out.

Pamela Coren

St Pancras' Well

Losing the true path
we climb a fence and drop,
braking against our rough descent.
Across the road, a track
promises completion of our quest,
but leads instead
to Washford River, rushing
and tumbling over shallow pebbles.

Shoulders brushing Himalayan Balsam
to wild explosions of seed,
we come upon a tiny beach
and sit for lunch,
watching sun-gold oak leaves
turn with the current,
sweeping the island's shingle tip
past spearmint's clutching roots.

Restored, we seek again the well,
trying to match with map
road, houses, stream and field:
at last we understand
the chapel changed to house
and holy well,
in tidy over-tended garden,
lost to us.

We thought to dip our fingers
in that sacred spring,
leave wave-smooth pebbles
as Ellen's offering
but now we turn away.

Yet disappointment fades,
and what remains
is the sparkling river curve,
rosy flush of balsam at our back,
an oak tree's eddying leaves
and between our finger tips
the fragrant crush of mint.

Heather Deckner

TOW ROPE

My father laid down his claw hammer,
took a rope from his truck

and lashed me to a chimney stack
on a half-nailed roof.

Nine jets in diamond pattern,
thundered over a boy's dizzy head

until they broke, to a starburst
in blue, white and red.

On glass at the edge of dawn,
we fished for roach and silver bream;

quietly, as if in prayer,
I watched him, for the slightest quiver.

When I made the school six,
he carved a chess set in American oak.

On the eve of my eighteenth,
he wept; sorry we hadn't been close.

A year or so later, he hung on to the rope
when the old truck was sold.

John Scarborough

On Omaha Beach

Then put out the lights and look again, this time further west
to Omaha and see there not the shimmering tide
but ravenous seas incarnadine with bodies
forming rafts up to the land until the beach
stands as if it were red set of sun
and not the dawn. The mother ships
lie too far out to shell the shore-line
batteries and men put out with packs
too much for easy movement
or to swim. So like shooting
apples in a barrel foreign
guns pick them off
and each man
takes a corner
of the sea
to wrap
about him.

She is thinking of his infancy
when his play was prayer
in the folds of fields
in Idaho among the corn
and byres, the slow duskfall
of voices.
The far-away door
of his youth slides open
and glides wide for him.

I will not share the sound
of your voice now
but keep it to my ear
to answer the old questions.

Are you hungry?
Are you warm enough?

The new ones
break along a shore
wearing pebbles thin.

Bones – baroque pearls –
the architecture of love –

the domes of pleasure –
the hues of grief –
sea bleached to stones –

Angela Brodie

SUMMER EVENING PARENTS

Blackbirds carol and consternate to sleep,
there's a cud cud of last tennis in the parks,
town traffic fizzes, seethes up from the heap
and dies into the sky like firework sparks.
A frenzy interweaves the doming trees –
a kid with a whistle, a scooter scream, harm
whined out of emergency across, oh please,
some tangent to us.

She sleeps. There's been a storm.
A warm mist rises – exhaling of brute world.
I'd make that whistling kid exhale, I say –
brash. Another noise that's swirled
about her perfect ear.

Up there, all ways away,
gaseous noises dissipate, world uncloaks;
no limit echoes … endless outward suck.
I draw her from the void above the oaks,
feel something sharp but empty pluck
at our thinned circumference. I face
its onomatopoeia for Liebestod.
But her sleep is nuclear core, yes-trace,
the given, the only lasting, nod.

Richard Smith

CABIN BED

Five years ago we sent you away
to your friend Lina's so we could install
a flat pack cabin bed.

Never OK with change, you set sail
from a low single awash with cuddlies
to a tall ship on the high seas.

It was a trial to build. Tempted
to bodge with the drill, we wisely
read the leaflet one more time,

so you weren't folded into white walls
one turbulent night, as if crushed
inside an origami boat.

You took up your elevated place,
spent wakeful hours of night alone,
and all the time you changed –

large bones, hair fuzzing your shins,
the bed creaked under your new weight
like timbers in a storm, and so, abruptly,

this huge structure, desk, bed, wardrobe,
shelves and ladder, colourful jetsam
of plastic, fossils, ribbons, feathers,

must now be washed away again.
In the empty room, the askew mattress
lies like a raft after the wreck,

guano-coated cliffs of scribbling paper
shelved into the recycling bin,
or to the memory box, to be forgotten.

You move to the loft, a crow's nest,
double bed rigged up for future voyages,
childhood stowed secretly below.

Clare Starling

Undercurrent

Realisation that he's not playing but panicking bolts
through me, and before I can think I am running over sand
from soft to hard, to water's edge, hitting the cold sea
in up to my knees and thighs, launching forward
into a head-up breaststroke, calling out, *I'm nearly there.*

He grabs hold as I reach him, clinging with arms and legs, head
pushed into my neck, part sobbing, part laughing. I tread water
to calm him, feeling the undertow, reassure that we'll swim back
to safety together, so ask him to kick with me against the current
tugging at us, *kick kick kick*, I say, *to help me get back.*

Kick kick kick, I say, like I used to say when he was learning to swim,
kick kick kick, as hard as you can. I'm doing side-stroke, my face
towards him
as I intone *kick kick kick* and as we approach the shore I see my older son
is in the water swimming towards us. No sooner have I landed
the younger one, I have to turn back and rescue his brother.

All this while their dad with our friends have been sitting on the beach
above the water line observing: their unconcern disconcerting
though no one has come to any harm. The kids huddle close, wrapped
in towels, no chatting. The dads joke about the land speed record
I probably broke, how I seemed to have it all in hand.

I think of this now: now that I no longer have two sons.
My younger child is swimming against the current again,
in a new way, in her brave way, moving to the truer version
of herself. I had never expected this. Here I am, waiting, held
at arms' length, watching, in fear of her drowning.

Sarah J Bryson

CATCH A WAVE

poolulating plurl
undulating
ooling swirl
glossfroth circles
uncertain seamotive
waiting waist high

frown,
ticshadow
swirlpool face
planesmooth suckripple
drawback undertow

swellsensors
alertfeel
here it
comes
rising
feet off the bottom
Ride High
Ride Easy
SOAR
RIDE FREE

CRASHCRESCENT

Smashpebble dumpbuttock, toebend bottomthump,
scratchleg thighpain, lowdump rumpache

rushrunnels, water absconded

a coarsegrit
stranding
an undignified
crawl to

STANDING.

Keith Willson

HOKUSAI'S GREAT WAVE AT THE HAMMERSMITH FLYOVER

I fill the tank / feel the empty
feel in the night a wave about
to break / feel the door shut
I feel empty / fill the tank

I see the light in the shop
hear the flyover traffic
feel the slippery concrete
feel the nozzle cold in my hand
my mind runs over / and over

us setting up the flat / crockery
ironing board / making
the bed I won't sleep in tonight
rest one hundred miles away
the flat door closed. I feel

flattened / cold / sunk
panic prayer rises to hold
back the wave risen above
the flyover / the cars / my journey
ready to wash me across
the forecourt / past the point
we knew would come / past

the shop where the cashier dreams
while CCTV flicks
camera / to camera
no petrol stink in her dreams
camera / to camera
sun on her nightshift skin

she starts awake / senses the weight
the reared wave.

Marius Grose

A Conversation with a Pillar Holding Up the M32 Motorway
(Junction 2)

Jesus Saves Jesus Saves Jesus Saves
is stencilled on you and I spray underneath
'But he still can't afford a house in Bristol.'

What do you think you're doing young man?

'I'm recalibrating the dynamics of intergenerational wealth,' I say.

You're full of big words aren't you?

'It's more of an aesthetic impulse,' I say, furtively
rolling the can in my hand, like a giant fag butt.

Kerthunk, kerthunk, kerthunk, it says.

'What's that?' I ask. 'I don't quite understand.'

*Have you never read The Translators's Guide to
The Gutteral Utterances of Transport Infrastructure?*

'No,' I say, looking guiltily at my sneakers,
'all they ever taught us at school was Houseman
and how to get a reasonable job in unreasonable times.'

Boom, kerthunk, trumble, scraw.

'But I'm trying,' I say, 'I really am.
I've listened to the soft tick of dusk streetlamps,
abandoned fridges, polystyrene coffee cups strung
between electric pylons. But the vernacular never rings true.'

Kethunk, brang, ricket tung, barolt, hush young man, it adumbrates,
*Listen more, listen through the crystalline catacombs of my crunching
bones.*

I drop my spray can and hear the single ring
of the apostrophe club, of the clanger, on the muted alarm.

Listen more, listen between the cars, listen from heartbeat to heartbeat.

And I hold my heart in my breath and then I hear it.

The river beneath the M32, where fish once leapt brilliantine
in the unshadowed sun, where kingfishers pierced the eye of dawn,
where stones rang in the bushel of old money and the pond weed
was as green as the first day of school.
'I can hear it,' I say, 'but it is so hard to hear. Someone is tapping
at my breastbone like a bailiff with a table leg.'

Don't turn away, don't... says the pillar.

But already it is too late. I watch the kids
surf the wooden ramps on their skateboards,
racing towards a future
they cannot see.

Jet McDonald

CRUSH

A seethe of boys
launched from the coach
& there we were
roasting in the ruins
of a Roman villa
brushed out from downland.
Amphoras. Jewellery.
Dominic's eyes
glazed with boredom
in the bathhouse,
its never-ending drought,
its tumble of rubble.
Then more mosaics showing off.
He flicked a *v* behind Miss Briscoe's back.
Made us laugh. Would rather spin some hours
glistening in the penny arcade.

We sat on the buzz cut grass,
snarling into Tupperware sandwiches
& sticky chocolate bars.
School ties drunk with heat.
On the coach home
the Sussex countryside blurred itself
through handprint windows.
Dom drifted,
his gladiator head
coming to rest on my shoulder.
I hoped this moment
would be captured
on thousands of brilliant tiles
I could hide deep in the chalky soil.
Then wait for the future
to discover us.

Simon French

The Peaceful Transfer of Power

Polling Station signs crack in a wind
that is turning trees inside out.
Greying wardens of the vote,
bristle with three-inch pencils,
scalpel sharp, ruling lines through names
double-checked, everything done just right.
Democracy smells of church halls,
sounds like voters scratching crosses,
and Big Ben's ten o'clock closing chimes.

Election nights are fever dreams,
county-show rosettes, fancy dress.
Someone or other, the something party,
thirteen thousand one hundred and two,
cheers, speeches that no one hears.
We do change well, when there is none.
Like Kings rising at a dead Queen's last breath,
ministers' house moves are delivered
with brute, unnecessary, pleasing haste.

But this could all disintegrate.
While staff change sheets, clear breakfast things,
it might be darkness entering No. 10's door,
leading off incumbents to shouts of *shame*,
pulling stubby pencils from polling booth strings,
parading demagogues through town halls,
exulting in our nervous sweat,
emptying ballot boxes into streets, ruining
the final election night's restless sleep.

Tom Ratcliffe

IN PARLIAMENT
(after Robert Henryson 1425 – 1506)

Henryson calls in his beasts. The unicorn
shot out his voice full shrill and gave a shout
and so they come – the leopard, minotaur,
the werewolf, Pegasus, the lynx,
tyrant Tiger, doggies all diverse,
polecats, ferrets, dromedary,
women and men, mice in the walls.
Scratching for food, digging the dead,
raging complaint, hissing contempt.
Old Lion Law can roar, but in the chamber stink
all beasts and men must dread the fetch,
foot it anxious and febrile round the floor,
tongues loosing slippy jargons at the box.
The fox, the fox, will not be stinted yet.

Pamela Coren

One Basket

Since the fox carried her siblings away,
she no longer laid in her usual spot.

I had to hunt them down, one by one:
under the glass of the cucumber frames;

out in the field where the alpacas hummed;
half-buried in the bran-tub like a lucky dip.

Evenings, I'd find her hiding in the hay-loft
then carry her to the hen-house

with its reinforced door. I'd stroke
the softest feathers at the back of her neck

till she made that throaty cluck
I took for affection.

She lived a long and petted life, though
she never relaxed her tactics.

Often I'd find an egg gone cold
too risky to use. Some mornings

running late, cows still to milk,
I'd curse as I frisked the farmyard

while she would stalk past like a stranger
her unblinking eye refusing clues.

Elaine Ewart

Under the Lea

The Lift

When Jeremy Clarkson offered me a lift from the poetry reading, I didn't have the heart to refuse. It was a lousy night and my mate with the car was trying to score with a young woman he hadn't seen before. She was talking, animatedly, about Sylvia Plath and giving Ted Hughes a hard time. He was agreeing, naturally. He wasn't a natural charmer, it was a compulsion, a habit. He nodded, but gestured me away. Nothing would come of it, but he'd keep on trying. I'd missed the last bus and Clarkson said he was going my way. I knew him vaguely, he attended when his schedule allowed but he'd never read anything. I think he just wanted to show off his new motor; a fair deal as far as I was concerned. I get a lift, he mouths off. Why me – I had no idea? It couldn't be any worse than playing bar billiards with Freddie Truman. So, I got in the car, or rather, I fell in. I didn't think I'd ever get out of that seat, unaided. Clarkson got in the other side; he was purring before he even started the engine. Then it was all leather and lights and knobs and levers to me. It was nice to look at, if you didn't know what it was. I did recognise the steering wheel and the gear stick, it was level with my shoulder. Clarkson speaks: *The thing you need to know about a car, is that they're just like a woman.* Then he takes off. The dials going frantic; revs, mph, other stuff. He was explaining his metaphor; talking about Simone de Beauvoir and someone called Julia Kristeva but I didn't take it all in. I was maxed out with language. I asked him if he was worried about speed cameras: *No, it was good PR, and you have to think about your image, constantly. It keeps the bread on the table.* Then he said: *"To be honest, for getting around town, I'd prefer a Fiat Panda or a Ford Fiesta. You can't park these things. So the fines are a problem too, if you pay them. But there we are. It's all marketing and agents. Image again. Poetry is an escape. We're all the product of fate.*

He stopped at the lights on Temple Street. A wolf walked in front and stared over the long bonnet, nodding at Clarkson. A wolf on his hind legs, quite the country gentlemen, I thought, in a Brown Barbour jacket, brown cavalry twills and a brown flat cap. There were no shoes (they would have been brown brogues, hand tooled). There was six inches of fur covered leg (brown) and paws. It was a wolf. *I have to go,* said Clarkson, unclipping his seatbelt and opening the door. An afterthought, he leaned back in: *You can have the car. They'll only give me another one.* The wolf was waiting by the newsagents. A horn was blaring as I walked around to the driver's side. The lights were on green. I waved to the driver behind and shrugged my shoulders. I put it in gear and slowly released the clutch. It moved off smoothly. There was no one outside the newsagents. *Clarkson's gone off with a wolf* I said to myself. But then there was another voice inside my head, or outside the car, I didn't know? It wasn't my story now. *All writers are thieves,* said the voice.

Dave Foxton

Dream Catcher 51

SIX PRINTS

I once knew an artist
who had a tempestuous relationship
with her vacuum cleaner.

The Moses baskets had already left.

A graceful surname and a missing father
grew into colour prints.

The twins spoke in rhyme.

*Twice you broke it, Hoover,
when you threw it down the stairs.*

Six framed prints, she left with me.
People wanted them, but they weren't mine to give.
The last one was a leafy scene, shadows sunlight and green.
The kids had written.

*Monster Harry lives in the woods, him dead now.
We go seaside morrow aren't we?*

Barbara Howerska

DREAM OF A SON
(after Eavan Boland's 'The Dream of Lir's Son':
'Indeed when in secret forms, dreams
Mime and play the future's mystery')

in the dream a basket floats
upon a sacred river

snags
on bullrushes where flotsam idles
beside lurid algae   dead beetles
and drifts of belly-up fish

ragged birds   fluffing out their oily feathers

he might
have been a future king

but already
he's spent his cache
of simoleons and emerald scarabs

and crawls alone from the river's
selvedge

in the dream he's my son
not mine exactly
but the only one gifted
to me

the one who is as he is now   a presence
in the world of women

loved as solidly
as a tree

as leafily as a pool is deep

he'll be   as he is now
undreamt

as he is   not was   or will become
unscripted

I say to the dream   *so he is not a myth*

Dream Catcher 51

the lost gold of shipwrecks
  a giallo/slasher song

night's white-boned trees
arching towards a thin unsmiling moon?

he's manga-literate   and likes
his pizza delivered by motorbike

I've no idea what plastic he'll find
in the lids cupboard

I say to the dream   *what is a son mean to be?*

a zebra owl   quiet
among the crowded screeching?

I ask the dream
why are fables irrelevant?

   so he is not a king
with fistmele   spiked shield   quiver

he will not
part a sea's immortal waters
or swim to shore from a washed-up story . . .

he is all I have ever wanted   but
he is a stranger
and as a stranger

what does he   the dreamer   think of me?

Jennifer Harrison

The Good Worker

The summertime fairground further along the loch is shut down like a marriage that's over, no movement on the roller-coaster. Katie says, "I'm glad we came. No-one else is feeding the birds."

Stuart says, "It's too cold for many people to be about. When you go to Mrs Hendry, don't mention what we fed the birds."

"It would have poisoned me and then she's murdered me."

The big open-sided shelter gives only an illusion of protection against the icy wind off the loch. Still, illusions help. Within the shelter, a conglomeration of birds stands patiently near the picnic table.

"It was just a bit of mould. She was just trying to be kind. She finds this Christmas cake she bought last year. She thinks, 'I know, I'll give it to Stuart and Katie, it'll save them having to get one.' That's being nice."

"She says I could have been her little girl if God meant her to have a little girl. I'm *not* her little girl. I'm Mummy's. She's telling a *lie*."

A woman walking a French bulldog fixes a stare on Stuart that lets him know she's filed him as an abductor or worse. The dog reminds him that Katie has been clamouring for a dog.

"Hello, birds," Katie says. She's put her little pink rucksack on the picnic table. She unpacks Mrs Hendry's Christmas cake and breaks it up. The carpet of birds flows towards her.

He says, "What Mrs Hendry said, it's just her way of saying she's fond of you. And that's good. We need to keep her on side, okay? To look after you while I'm doing my shifts. If I have to pay for childcare…" His shrug brings a reminder of how ineffective against the cold his thin summer zip-up jacket is.

"She keeps kissing me. Her eyes are another person looking through her glasses. She keeps saying Mummy's not coming back."

"Just tell her we gave them stale bread."

"That's telling lies. I cut the mould off so the birds won't get poisoned. They can leave the icing if they don't like it."

"People leave me because they don't like me."

"What did you say, Daddy?"

"Nothing."

"Yes, you did, Daddy, so you told a lie." She aims fragments of cake towards birds. "No, it's not for you, it's for him. You wait your turn. You throw some, Daddy. It's fun."

"I'm not allowed fun." He makes his voice feeble and wavery. "The doctor said fun brings on the purple habdabs."

"That's for *you*," she calls, throwing cake in the direction of a blue-tit on the fringe. "And that's for *you*, Rihanna Robin." The intended recipients fly up in alarm at hostile missiles; unintended birds get the dole. "No, just *wait*. It's unfair to take other people's. Little birds get their share first. – Oh, that pigeon. He's..."

It stands on one foot, sometimes fluttering its wings to keep upright. The other leg ends in a stump, clawless.

"Oh, poor Peter Pigeon. How did it happen?"

"It'll have got it caught in something."

She throws cake towards the one-legged pigeon but other birds swoop in and scuffle. A big seagull flies off with it. "It's for Peter Pigeon!" Katie calls angrily. "That seagull, it's had three pieces already. He's greedy." She tiptoes towards the pigeon, hand forward with cake. It doesn't perceive her yearning to succour it and flutter-hops away towards a stand of other pigeons. "You're silly. I'm trying to help you. You deserve justice." The cake she throws it is pecked up by one of the others. "Daddy, Peter's disabled but the others don't treat him with dignity and respect."

"It's nature, Katie."

"Nature is horrible." She looks helplessly at Stuart with tears in her eyes.

"Look, darling girl, we need to get home. My shift at Pam's Delidelicious starts at 2." He puts a finger to her cheek. "You're getting cold, too. Just scatter the rest of the cake."

As she does so, she wails, "The seagull's coming back."

"Glad to see someone's coming back." Stuart only mutters it but Katie says, "What did you say, Daddy?"

"Nothing."

"You did, Daddy. 'Nothing' was telling a lie."

"Katie, don't keep accusing your Dad of lying."

He does not add, "Taking after your mother."

He says it. Then he shouts, "Get the fuck away," and runs at the seagull, waving his arms, and of course all the birds take flight.

She's clutching her pink rucksack like a baby monkey clinging to a mother-substitute. Her cry of "Oh" sounds like pain at first, but no, it's a cry of ecstasy as she abandons the rucksack, runs from the shelter to kneel before a golden Labrador puppy on a lead. It's new to life and leaping and licky. Mud on the knees of her dungarees, clean on an hour ago – it'll be too late (consideration for neighbours) to put them through the machine when he gets in tonight – could he ask Mrs Hendry...?

"She'll take him off your hands," Stuart jokes to the austere-looking man in a long comfortable officer coat who's walking the puppy.

"If it were up to me. My wife might have other ideas."

As they walk on, Katie says, "Oh, Daddy, I would love him ever so, a puppy like that."

"We've to find the deposit for your school trip first. I think we'll manage it, thanks to Mrs Hendry getting you a nice winter coat. See, she's kind."

"I hate it. It's all big and puffy."

"If Pamela Wishart will give me more shifts, we'll see. That's the best I can say. If I get extra shifts, Mrs Hendry'll have to have you more often.

So if she asks if you liked the cake, don't tell her we fed it to the birds. We can't afford to upset her."

She might be upset, too, by being asked to look after a puppy as well as Katie.

Katie halts in a pose of thinking. "I'll tell her it was lovely."

"Wouldn't that be a wee lie, hen?"

"The birds thought it was lovely."

***

The doors of Pam's Delidelicious are wide open to the street, and its smell, hinting in summer of a subtle feast, is shrivelled by cold to a memory of cheese. Behind her circular counter, above glass-fronted shelves of meats and salads, cheeses and pies, Maggie huddles in a big puffy anorak.

"Why don't you shut the doors?"

"Pamela–prefers–them–open." Maggie's speaks slowly. She's here without wages under a work experience scheme for people who are disabled or long-term sick.

Stuart touches her cheek behind her lank hair. "You're perished, hen. You'll catch your death." Does she have a reduced life-expectancy anyway? But that's how you speak to ordinary people.

Martin watches from behind the ill-lit corner counter for booze.

Stuart adds, "There are laws about temperatures in workplaces. Your breath is vapourising."

Maggie turns so she can't be seen from the door to the backshop. She raises a gloved finger to her lips. She moves her eyes warningly towards the door. It's not quite shut, trembling in the frame as though shivering.

"I'm not cold," calls Martin. His sweater sleeves are down over his hands. Whenever he speaks, he smiles like a friend. His face and dark goatee could be on a brand label for luxurious eatables.

In the backshop, where Stuart will spend most of his shift, there's nose-clogging warmth from a fan-heater and radiator. The warmth emphasises the doggy smell from Pamela Wishart's cairn terrier in its basket. It's a snappy beast and doesn't like other dogs, so if Katie gets a dog there's no chance of bringing it into work with him. Pamela Wishart is engrossed in paperwork at her desk. When Stuart says, "Chilly day," she looks up as if surprised to see him.

"Stuart! You were saying about wanting more shifts."

"Now it's just me and Katie, yes."

"The thing to do, Stuart, is to reflect. On what might make management call you in more often. You're a good worker, I grant you that." She gives him a very caring smile. "But Martin could do with more shifts, too."

He hangs his summer jacket, checks labels on a stack of large cartons, heaves a carton onto a table, starts opening it.

After a while, as though it's of no moment, he says, "Could we shut the front doors? Maggie's freezing."

"I prefer them open."

"Why?" He sounds merely and chattily curious.

"I prefer them open."

He's taking out packets of Swedish cinnamon biscuits.

"Why?"

Her faces creases with anguish. "I, personally, wish we could close them. But open doors is a business decision every shop in the street has made. Welcoming customers. No shifts at all for you, let alone extra ones, if we don't welcome customers."

"Other shops' doors have, like, this curtain of hot air."

Her voice addresses the better nature she just knows he has. "Squandering precious environmental resources to send warm air out into the cold! Destroying the planet!"

"Look, just come with me."

She puts on her listen-to-your-staff face. In her black pin-striped trouser suit that strains across her stomach, she follows Stuart into the shop. He grabs one of her hands, holds it against Maggie's face. "Feel that."

There's movement at the shop entrance, a buggy, a woman pushing it in. "I'm looking for Italian figs in chocolate my friend got here. Gorgeous."

Maggie sets off tottering towards the wall shelves where Stuart stacked them yesterday, but Pamela says, "Could you get them for the customer, Stuart, please?" As he ascends the little wooden stepladder with the tall support pole, Pamela gives the customer a wry look, shaking her head, as if inviting agreement on men's thoughtlessness.

Martin smiles from among the fine wines.

"With her buggy, would she have come in if the doors hadn't been open?" Pamela muses when she and Stuart are in the backshop again. She laughs in intimation that what follows is entirely friendly. "When I was in HR, I had to deal with someone who complained that grabbing someone's wrist and pulling them about was an assault. I had to issue a formal warning."

"The thing is" – he's slitting an empty loukoumi carton along the sides with a scissors blade, collapsing it flat – "when you think of Maggie's condition, her difficulties... What is it she has?"

There's good-humoured exaggeration in Pamela's voice as she replies, "Data protection! Confidentiality! It's more than my business is worth to breathe a word about Maggie's medical history. Let's just be glad she's being supported into employment, treated with dignity and respect as we provide work experience. We mustn't patronise her by treating her differently from ordinary staff."

From out in the shop come the sounds of footsteps, of more voices.

Stuart throws down the scissors, runs back into the shop, mounts the stepladder to the little platform at the top, clutches the tall support pole, leans out over the customers like a ship's figurehead. "Ladies and gentlemen, your attention, please."

They all look up: a man and a woman watching Maggie laboriously cut a slice of quiche; two guys, probably students, examining health bars on Martin's counter.

Stuart calls, "Cold in here, isn't it?"

"Isn't it?" he insists, a preacher in a pulpit demanding responses.

The quiche-buying woman says, but to the man, "It is, isn't it?"

One of the students calls, grinning, "Yes."

"And people like Maggie here have to work in this freezing cold all day long every day."

Maggie gives a radiant smile. Pamela Wishart is through from the backshop, her face expressionless beneath shaggy girls'-night-out hair. Stuart continues, "Are you okay with that?"

"Shut the doors, then," snaps the quiche-buying man.

"Ah, but the doors mustn't be shut. Why? Because they think you, the customers, are thickos. Unless the doors are wide-open, giving Maggie pneumonia, you won't realise, 'Here's a shop, it sells stuff I want.'"

One of the students holds up a mobile.

"Great," Stuart calls. "Put this on social media."

Pamela Wishart steps up close to the mobile, blocking its view. "Film me, if you must. As proprietor with a duty of care, I cannot allow one of my staff with cerebral palsy to be put on social media."

The boy puts the mobile away but says to Pamela Wishart, "She's still cold."

"Maggie," Pamela coos, in a voice to be heard by all, "don't you remember what I said? When you feel the cold, just pop through to the backshop for a warm. I'll always cover for you." The customers see her smile at Maggie with pity and love. To the woman, as if they are friends chatting, Pamela adds, "It's been impossible getting someone to come and look at the heating."

There's a crack from the tall pole Stuart is gripping as he leans down to focus his indignation towards Pamela. "You told me not to phone a heating engineer." The quiche-buying woman calls up to him, "Are those jars behind you cherries?"

"Fuck the fucking cherries," says Stuart, and there's a splintering sound as he falls to the floor, still clutching the tall pole. The man – he's in a long comfortable officer coat – Christ, it's the man who walked the puppy at the loch – hands Pamela a card, saying, "If he sues for compensation, I'll be a witness for you."

Pamela Wishart sounds regretful on Stuart's behalf. "I'm afraid he was not up that ladder in the course of his employment duties. This is his last day with us. We've been bidding him farewell with a lunchtime drink. Perhaps he took one or two too many, ha-ha."

The students seem about to put back on Martin's counter the things they'd been going to buy. "Have them with our compliments," Pamela says. They laugh as they exit with them.

Dream Catcher 51

Struggling to his feet, Stuart says to the man and woman, "Why don't you leave, too? Show you're decent people, not prepared to patronise a place that treats poor Maggie like shit."

To the woman, Pamela Wishart says, as if confiding an intimate secret, "That quiche is made with a lovely tangy Spanish cheese. It's *my* favourite." That it's her favourite, says her voice, must be a strong recommendation. "Have your slice as a sample. On the house." She smiles them out of the shop.

When Stuart emerges from the backshop to leave Pam's Delidelicious for the last time, Martin is across talking to Maggie. Stuart fully detaches the pole from the stepladder. They watch him like he's a dangerous creature who might turn on them.

Outside, Stuart zips up his jacket that's almost useless against the cold – no chance of a winter one now – and pulls the shop doors shut behind him. He lodges the broken-off stepladder pole between the two bow handles so that the doors will be shut for quite a time.

Paul Brownsey

HAZEL TIME
(after John Berryman's 'Dream Songs')

There she was day in day out greenoveralled
a little stout a little frightening I learned
not   at all. We never saw a him   just her
out front bagging up the veg and fruit
to queues and queues of purseclasped women
and errand runners on Saturdays.

It was a wonder   all the other world knew more
what lay behind the potatoes pears in boxes
pine bare front shop soily floor and till   where
was her other life   her other clothes her hair
within the turban the inside out   not
just the where-with-all for green-grocering?

Imagining her unhappy come hazel time
I got let in to   well I never did   and sweet
Audrey shone   smile unhid sunned curls
and plumped in pink jumper with nails all shiny
and slim with a him   and a girl and boy
and cake   besides   around   the square table.

Angela Brodie

Pas De Deux

Three months after my accident, I started riding my bike again. To and from work, an easy route, mostly through the city's parks. It was summer. Long days. Bare legs. I was alive, regaining my strength, still in a job; I should have been feeling good. But each day when I locked my bicycle in the underground car park I felt as heavy as the building above me. I had to force my body up the stairs, unable to face the lift. Up I climbed, one leaden foot after the other, to the fourteenth floor, to my cubicle, where I sat and stared at the screen and made my fingers clatter across the keyboard. Eight hours later, my senses dulled, I rode through a green blur, relying on my bicycle to coast me safely home.

At first, I didn't realise I was being followed. In the mornings, once I'd crossed the bridge, I cut through side streets to reach the long sweeping avenues and the cool hush of the city's lungs. After a few days, I became aware that somewhere in those side streets a skateboarder fell in behind me. A quiet whoosh-whoosh, which was not my bicycle, shadowed me through the park, then faded away in the short frenetic crisscrossing of roads that led to my workplace. In the evenings, too, I was vaguely conscious of a figure gliding into my slipstream at the edge of the park, dropping away again before the bridge.

I wondered whether I should feel threatened. There were so many things that the rational side of my brain was telling me I *should* feel, but that I didn't. When I was cycling, I knew that I was alive in a way that I did not when I was logged onto the PC at work. But it was scant knowledge. As I cycled, my muscles contracted and released, my blood circulated, the tips of my fingers no longer felt numb. Then the knowledge drained away as I locked my bike once more in the underground car park. To feel threatened, I reasoned, you had to have something worth losing.

One evening, as I reached the top of the ramp up from the basement, I caught sight of my stalker. He was half my age, at least, a moody beanpole, hanging around by the news-stand opposite the office block, hopping on and off his skateboard with jerky, twitchy movements, his hands shoved in the pockets of his low-slung jeans.

I turned left into the busy road and heard a thwack as the skateboard and rider landed on the tarmac several metres behind me. I rode hard, darting in and out of the traffic, taking risks I hadn't dared to since my accident, and, to my surprise, enjoying the fumy air and the blast of engine-fuelled noise. All the way to the park the lights were in my favour, and then I slackened off, freewheeling until that gentle whoosh-whoosh swung into range of my hearing. I pedalled just enough to maintain an easy distance between us. As I exited the park, the soft trundling of the skateboard trailed away into the side streets.

For a week or more we continued our remote pas de deux. In the mornings he tucked in behind me seemingly from nowhere. I varied my route a couple of times but he still found me. Every evening when I left work he was there by the news-stand, chin to chest, shoulders hunched. Graceless until he was on his skateboard, weaving and shimmying behind me. I caught glimpses as I turned a corner or checked the traffic over my shoulder; a flickering, slender figure, the slightest swivel of his hips swerving his board this way and that. Sometimes during the day I found myself staring up at the window instead of at my screen, wondering what he got up to while I tapped in monotonous data. A warning flashed up on my screen: SESSION IDLE OVER 3 MINUTES. AUTOMATIC LOG OFF COMMENCES IN 15 SECONDS.

One morning I woke to the sound of rain. The scar that zigzagged down my right leg ached. When the rain finally eased, I got up and put on my cycle gear. I would be late, and reprimanded. I set off in the drizzle, my legs stiff and heavy. Cycling over the bridge I breathed deeply, trying to dampen the flutters of panic multiplying inside me. Then, two streets away from the park, the swoosh-swoosh of skateboard wheels on wet tarmac crept up behind me. The heaviness dissolved from my limbs. I glided into the park, into the giddy scents of wet grass, fresh mulch, flowers opening to the soft rain, and realised I was smiling.

Exiting the park, I checked over my shoulder. His hood was up, though the drizzle had all but petered out by now. I slowed down, hoping to catch every red light. By the time I reached the top of the ramp I was weighed down with dread again. I pressed the button on the video intercom and asked reception to let me into the car park. The roller door at the bottom of the ramp began to trundle up. I pumped my brakes, controlling the short descent so as to pass under the door without having to duck.

I pedalled reluctantly across the half empty car park, the roller door cranking closed behind me. The bicycle rack was at the far end, under a flickering fluorescent light. Two crumpled bikes, at either end of the rack, hadn't shifted in all the time I'd been working there. I locked my bike and unhooked my panniers. Only then, beneath the continuous low roar of the air conditioning system, did I hear the swish of a skateboard. He'd followed me in. A tickle, like a brief electric shock, ran up the length of my scar. Crouched down on his board, he wove between the parked cars, ignoring me, his lips pursed together in concentration. I watched for a moment, and then turned and headed to the stairs, and the long climb up to my cubicle.

For once, the day flew past. I accepted the reprimand for lateness from my boss with contrition, much to her consternation. Evidently she had expected, hoped for, a confrontation, a chance to humiliate me. 'Well, don't make a habit of it,' she said half-heartedly, sending me back to my cubicle. I settled straight into my work, completing each new task that popped up on my screen with quick facility, my fingers dancing across the keyboard. I didn't need to stare up at the window and wonder. Fourteen storeys below, my weekday shadow practised spins and flips and kickturns. He guarded my bicycle. The knowledge that he would be there, skulking in a dark corner, when I descended the stairs at the end of the day, buoyed me up through the intervening hours.

The underground car park welcomed me, with its hum of machinery, its stench of petrol and stale piss. The slight tremor in my right leg told me he was present. As soon as I'd snapped my cleats into the pedals and started for the roller door he was skating behind me, building momentum for the run up the ramp. I pressed the button to retract the roller door, waited until it was three quarters open, and launched myself up the slope, into the late summer evening. He scooted tight on my back wheel, hunched down as low as possible, and passed beneath the security camera. Elation rushed through my veins and I rode recklessly, thrilling to his skill in tailing me through the traffic. Then the calm of the park, sunlight streaming through the trees, and a smoky hint of autumn in the air.

By the end of the following week my work rate had improved so dramatically that I was in danger of winning the Employee of the Month award. Data flowed effortlessly through me while my hooded angel wove his skateboard magic in the car park below. More than ever, I lived for the journey to and from work, the game of tag in which we never touched.

Friday morning was overcast, thunderstorms forecast. I was sticky with sweat before I reached the bridge, my cheeks burning. In the side streets, I had to dodge between lines of idling cars, and it was only once I was through to the park that I could be sure my chaperon had fallen in behind. He hung back, skimming lazily this way and that along the avenue, allowing for my sluggish pace.

Then I was back in the stalled traffic, edging between tightly packed cars and buses, buffeted by gusts of heat and fumes from impatiently revving engines, wishing I'd stayed in the park, riding the circuit of avenues forever.

A young woman dashed out into the road in front of me, nipping between two stationary cars. I swore and fought to retain my balance. From the same side of the road came jeering laughter, a mocking shout: 'Lucky saddle!' A moment later, skateboard and rider landed with a smack on the pavement, and my stalker, my protector, shoved the offending lout against the wall. 'Shut your mouth, loser,' he said coolly, and the flush of anger and embarrassment that had swamped me receded. I rode the last few hundred metres to work in a daze.

This time, he did not follow me down into the underground car park. My error rate went up, sparing me the indignity of the Employee of the Month award. Storm clouds rolled in across the city, dumped a month's worth of rain, scattered and dispersed eastwards. When I left at the end of the day he was hanging around by the news-stand, fidgeting his feet on and off the skateboard. In the park, the trees and grass and flowers all shimmered, smelling like freshly washed linen. We drifted out into the now quiet side streets and then he was gone.

Hilaire

Dietary Changes of the Woke Generation

A herd of almonds sweeps across the orchard.
Early fallers follow a path to the milking parlour,
with hooves of soft blossom and flanks of wrinkled hide,
shedding a lament for split halves, heading to be crushed.

They cross the field. They gather at the water trough
to wallow in liquid till they swell. Fat bellies float.
The nutherd tips them into a cavernous mortar,
pestles them smooth and wraps them in muslin.

The almonds drip, are wrung and wrung to drip more.
At last, their sacrifice can be bottled, translucent
as moonlight dancing on the domes of mushrooms,
their desiccated offal sent to marzipan factories.

The milkman's electric cart's hum and clink
threads the streets of Bohemian urbanites, waking
to the lactose-free tang of vegan cheese and yoghurt,
nut-milk percolating quinoa flakes and yuzu slices.

Sue Spiers

HERDWICK RAM

Today there's nothing doing down pheromone alley.
He strolls between ewes, sniffs their rims

with slim expectation – encrypted inside his primal brain,
a timetable that follows charts.

He's keeping his spirits up, savours the buttery scents,
lanolin notes, gamey highs that ghost promise

like a good vintage waiting to be pulled.
He rests his wool-thickened neck

along a dam's busy curves as she tugs with passion at silage.
His eyes dimmed, already half-way there.

Claire Booker

The Lamp Room

We stood in the kitchen as Zoe drew on her spliff and gazed into the distance. She ran one finger through her bright red hair then laid her hand on the strap of her dungarees. I shuffled from one foot to the other on the stone floor, uncomfortable being in this odd house with this woman I'd just met.

'Just you here?' I said.

She blew out a stream of smoke. 'It's just me. Me and my stuff.' She laughed and waved a hand around the room. There was a Welsh dresser, an Aga, a Belfast sink and a long table with benches on either side. The table was empty apart from a tray with a stained mug, a half-empty cafetière and an ashtray of roll-up stubs. On the dresser there were bottles of wine and spirits and shelves holding mismatched glasses.

'You want a drink?' she said.

'Yeah. Thanks.'

'Wine or beer?'

It was only four o'clock and drinking booze didn't seem the thing to do. Not when I was here to do a deal. But Zoe didn't seem the kind of person to care and I was taking the train home so one was probably fine.

'Beer, thanks.'

She went into the pantry and came out with a bottle of French beer, handing it to me with a bottle opener. She poured herself a glass of Chianti and I popped the lid on the beer, taking a sip. It fizzed in my mouth and made my eyes water but it tasted good and actually, some alcohol was probably just what I needed. I was still shaken from the drive to her house - I'd not expected her to meet me at the station in a red sports car and belt us along the lanes at break-neck speed.

'That's a nice car you have,' I said.

'It's a Lotus. It was my dad's.' She looked away. 'I suppose you want to see the camera.'

'Please.'

I took another swig of beer, then left the bottle on the table following her as she headed along a hallway. The house hadn't looked so big from the outside but it went back some way. We went up a wide staircase and stopped by one of the doors. Zoe fished out a key and fumbled with the lock while balancing her wine glass and spliff. The door to the room opposite was open. There were bare floorboards stained with paint and furniture covered in dirty sheets.

'We're doing the place up,' she said.

'Oh?'

'It was my grandmother's. Needs some work.'

She opened the door. There was a bay window with heavy shutters partially shut and a black-painted fireplace. Against the nearest wall was an old set of drawers. There were photographs hung up all around the room and at the far end, there was a long table with an Apple computer, a large printer and stacks of paper. The photos on the wall were hard to see in the dim light but they seemed to be distorted pictures of animals, some of them close up.

Zoe went over to the drawers, drew out a camera bag and unzipped it. 'Here you go.'

I took the bag. Inside was the Nikon she'd advertised, fitted with a lens and complete with a charger and spare battery.

'Want to try it?' she said.

'Please.'

I aimed the camera across the room. It was much heavier than the one I already owned. It focused quickly and I snapped a couple of shots. I adjusted the settings and took several more, then tried the flash and looked at the images on the rear screen.

'Does the lens come with it?'

'Everything in the bag,' She drew on the joint and blew smoke out through her nose. 'What kind of stuff do you do?'

'Landscapes. Unusual stuff.'

'Unusual?'

'Light painting. HDR. Long exposures.'

I put the camera down and took out my phone, finding the link to my website and handing it to her. She held her joint and glass of wine in one hand and flicked through the photos. I picked up the Nikon again, taking a few more shots.

'Seems fine,' I said.

'Try some more.'

I wandered out into the hall and across to the sash window. It faced the garden which was a mess of uncut lawns, shrubs and hedges. Putting the camera on the windowsill I undid the latch, yanking it against years of overpainting. The window slid up stiffly but held when it was fully open. I leant on the sill and aimed the Nikon, focussing on a beech tree at the far end of the garden. The camera locked on and took a shot. I tried several more, aiming at different parts of the garden and varying the settings.

There was a smell of dope smoke that let me know Zoe was behind me. 'What do you think?' she said.

'Seems good.'

'Hasn't had much use. It was a spare body. I've gone mirrorless.' She drew hard on the spliff and closed her eyes. When she opened them, they were rolled up for a second, like she was savouring the taste. She blew smoke out of the side of her mouth. 'So, what do you think.' There was something about her that had changed, softened. Maybe it was the joint or the wine. Both were nearly finished.

'I think I'll take it.'

She reached towards me, leant her body in close then extended one arm. Her other arm brushed against me as she pulled the window shut. She handed me my phone. 'I like your work.'

Then she walked across the hall, back into the room with the photos. I followed bringing the camera. The shutters were open and light filtered through the trees outside. She pulled a battered cash box out of a drawer in the desk.

'Sorry,' she said. 'Money stuff.'

I handed over the cash I had rolled up in my back pocket. 'It's all there.'

'Thanks.' She put it into the box without counting it. 'Want to look at my work?' She waved a hand towards the photos on the wall.

I went over to the nearest ones. They were dead animals - a cat, a pheasant and two I couldn't make out. Crushed and mangled. Walking around I saw that they were all dead, some splayed on the ground and others disfigured beyond recognition. Zoe watched me as I looked at the photos, another spliff in her mouth. There were all kinds of other animals: ducks and squirrels and a dog and a sheep and a fox. A deer and a badger. Others were too crushed or rotten to be identified, just a mass of hair and bones and decayed flesh. They were high quality, from a photography point of view. Perfectly focused, lit and framed but the content was hard to look at. Disgusting. I stopped at one of a deer, a blank eye staring out of its mangled head, teeth bared in a sneer.

'You like them?' Zoe was close behind me, her smoky breath on my neck.

'Yeah. They're amazing.' I didn't add how horrible they were. Revolting.

She came round and stood beside me, her arm touching mine. 'You want to see more?'

'Yeah.' I expected her to open a drawer or pull out a portfolio, but she left the room.

I followed as she led off down the stairs and along the passageway, back towards the kitchen but she turned left, down a few steps to a wooden door with peeling green paint. 'Prepare to be amazed.' She flicked a switch beside the door and light shone through cracks in the woodwork and gaps around the doorframe. 'You'll love this.'

When she opened the door light flooded out. There were more steps down to a room with a cobbled floor and shapes on the wall.

She led me in.

The wall was covered in skulls. Animal ones of different types and each had light bulbs mounted in their eye sockets. These were various sizes of bulbs to match the skulls they were paired with.

She came close to me, peering into my eyes. 'Do you love it?'

'Yeah,' I said, looking around. 'They are really something.' Which they were, but I wasn't sure I liked them at all.

'You think?' She went over to the doorway and flicked a switch.

The main lights went off, so the only illumination was from the bulbs in the eye sockets. There were different tints: blues and greens and reds and oranges.

She came over and held my sleeve. Her face was a distorted pattern of shadows. 'This is what it's about, don't you think?'

I nodded, unsure what to say.

'I have all kinds here. All kinds of animals. But there's one I'd like.' She laughed and put a hand on my forehead. Her skin was warm. Rough.

For a moment we stayed like that and she stared at me, concentrating on one eye at a time, her hand still on me. Like a blessing or something. She leaned a little closer and kissed me on the cheek. Then she drew back and went over to the door. I thought she was going to put the main lights on but she put the skull lights off. It was pitch black.

'Zoe?' I said. Something brushed against my hand and I stepped back, arms outstretched.

She laughed from somewhere behind me, so I moved the opposite way and stumbled on a step, dropping to my knee. I felt around in the dark to find the steps and door. Find my way out and away.

Then the skull lights came back on. Zoe hadn't moved away from the door. 'Don't they look amazing!'

The lamps seemed to dance around and were dazzlingly bright.

She noticed I was stooped down. 'Are you okay?'

'Just a bit dizzy.' The room spun around me. I was ready to leave. Get the hell out of the place. I straightened up and took a deep breath.

Her smile faded and she put the main light on. 'Maybe it's time to go.' She spun around and went back upstairs and I followed her and picked up the camera. She didn't speak as she led me to the car.

As soon as I was in, she started the engine, revving up and pulling off fast across the yard and down the lane.

It didn't take long to get back to the station but we travelled without speaking, the growl of the car's exhaust the only sound. She slammed the brakes on and parked where we'd met.

'Hope you like the camera,' she said, eyes fixed on the station building in front of us.

'I will, thanks.'

She nodded and messed with her hair band.

People walked past on their way to catch trains - a couple holding hands; a family of four with suitcases. Ordinary life.

Now we were back in the real world, the stuff with the lights and the skulls didn't seem so serious. Not so scary.

'By the way,' I said. 'I liked your work.'

She looked across at me. 'Yeah?'

'The photos were excellent.'

'Oh?'

'And the illuminated skulls were amazing.'

She leaned over towards me and opened the glove compartment. After fishing around she pulled out a card and gave it to me. The card had her name on it and her website address. There was a picture of one of the skull lamps in the middle.

'I'd better get my train.'

She snatched the card off me and grabbed a pencil from a door bin, writing a number on the back. 'Look me up.'

I slid out of the car and shut the door. The Lotus started with a bark and then she pulled off, swinging it around. She stopped and wound down her window as if to say something but then waved and drove off with a wheel spin.

Once the car's exhaust note had faded into the distance I went into the station, standing on the platform.

I looked up her website and flicked through the photos of mutilated animals, transfixed by their dead eyes. The empty eye sockets and crushed skulls. The mangled images that Zoe loved.

Ian Chapman

Between the Covers

My mother has found a place to thrive
inside the pages of War and Peace. She curls
up with Prince Andrei, who she knows
would love her as no other man has.

This morning at breakfast, Andrei dies
of gangrene in her arms. *If only he'd been born
fifty years later, the doctors could have saved him*,
she announces, hoping for a shoulder to cry on.

My father, the engineer, continues to dissect
his bacon with gusto: *Tolstoy had to bump him off
for the sake of the plot, love.* Mother goes
into mourning for the rest of the day.

Claire Booker

To A Spider

The bath's steep sides are prone to gravity,
exhausted you lurk in its deepest cavity.
Last night I helped you with a sheet of paper,
you scuttled, played dead,
then succumbed to my scraper.

You
  dropped

     on

        the

          carpet   then off you ran   [to some dark corner]
                but all in vain –

       this
       morning
       you're
      back
     in the
   bath
again.

I think that you're your own worst enemy
How can you have such limited memory?
What's the point of heroic struggle
if one careless
        morning
              you're washed
                      down
                           the
                              p
                                l
                                 u
                                  g
                                  h
                                  o
                                  l
                                  e
                                  ?

Keith Willson

Fly Trap

You swipe across my morning
        like a dry-wipe marker –
            not on the agenda,
        you invade my indoor shelter.
  I'm wrapped in my laptop
              leased out, on the clock –
                  your loose zoom riles
                      my back-to-back
timeslots.
              I'm inclined to roll the gazette
        smash you to a mess
          freaked by your yellowy insides
             your failure to survive –
        instead I sigh, take the time
            to pursue your buzz
                around my space
                    you loop back
            batter the flat glass,
      the open pane plain
    to my non-compound eyes –
  'til swirling air effects a breeze,
you lift out, freed –
  I'm left in place
      gazing after your trace
          life spiralling wild
              into the wide outside

Clare Starling

FIENDISH

A Tuscan cheese store,
its customs old as the quarried walls
and flagstone floors
that cooled its shadow air long

before refrigeration,
awaits a still older guest,
a timelessly ancient invader,
in the night of the long fangs.

The lead-off guy, let's call him Razor,
gnaws his way through the rind,
then burrows right into the core,
leaving a golfball-sized hole

about two inches from the floor
on a side facing a wall, where
no one would ever go rooting,
except, maybe, the rats.

He is followed by the rest,
shooting in, like Winston's incubus,
though this is no cage but a tunnel
and the intent is not to scare

but consume beyond all previous
notions of gorging, even if
the requisite patience is
undreamt of in our biology.

To that end the team must construct
a labyrinth of arteries, along which
they flow, one by one, in place of blood,
each of them trained to nibble

piano piano, just in case
an eagle-minded food inspector
passes this single column
of what should be prime parmesan –

as opposed to the perfect shell
it will become a week from now.

If you knocked on it then
the clang would be deafening

as a church bell struck in anger.
But the mission of eating's a trifle,
compared to the exit strategy.
First, they've made sure on entry

the tunnel's bigger than seems needed,
to allow for the swollen bulk
of the returning troops, whose blunted teeth
and long satiated appetite

would not bear the task of widening
on the way back. Then, just to fox
that putative passing nark
they do not scamper out, risking

the echo of multiple claws.
Instead the nimblest tiptoes down,
and drags the others through by the tails
with his teeth, all lying on their back.

*

Thus speaks an ex-*formaggiaio*
who suffered huge losses,
and had to change career,
relocate to London,

open a restaurant,
now a top ten pick,
but hardly sleeps a night without
dreams of the old foe.

Nick Cooke

EDITORS

They fuck you up some editors.
They may not mean to but they do;
Scour verse for all their favourite flaws
And dump the bloody lot on you.

But they've been fucked up in their turn
By dons alarmed at what they lack.
Rejections taught them what to spurn
When stabbing others in the back.

Misery delights in company.
Question their spurious commands.
Keep your originality
Don't put your work into their hands.

Dave Wynne-Jones

Wildfires

Of all the times to announce wildfires are sweeping across the carpet. That our basins gasp for water. Every heyday has its invoice my lover & we can't wipe time from a dirty clockface. It's still the same o'clock tocking in its same smoggy direction. The same tropic of bedroom in the same old postcode with hazard lights for entertainment. Heatwaving. Not sleeping. Mother Nature's banshee unleashes the full curdle of her repertoire & you need me to rustle up photographs of beautiful raincoats. Babies without sunblock. I know when you take a god, any god, fall to your knees & karaoke for all you're worth, that we've always been polar opposites melting in each other's arms, but we won't be dreamless. Today we should grill hoax meat. Let's turn malevolent circuitry into pauper knick-knack. Trap exhaust fumes in jars so our children's children can only breathe ghosts into the very Eden of their lungs. Know we did our best.

Simon French

REVIEWS

If you have a book you'd like reviewed, or know of one you think deserves a review, or want to write a review yourself, please send to me during the usual submission windows and to my address in Leeds (not to Stairwell in York) – see the website for full details. We cannot guarantee to review everything we receive.

Dancing About Architecture, Edited by Oz Hardwick and Cassandra Atherton
MadHat Press
ISBN: 978-1-952335-76-1 pp 256 $22.95

'Writing about music is like dancing about architecture'; this anonymous quotation forms the starting point for Hardwick and Atherton's ambitious and innovative project to represent the best in ekphrastic poetry, the subject of a conference chaired at Leeds Trinity University by Hardwick last year.

If you thought you knew what ekphrastic poetry was, or hoped to get a definitive fix on it – think again. Each poem is accompanied by an often meaty commentary of the poet's process/inspiration/background, in which some poets aim for analysis, while others are more reflective. One of the most striking aspects of this remarkable book is the diversity it represents, and the freedom with which the featured poets have responded to the brief. Every time you think you have found 'an answer' you turn the page and there is a totally different question.

Some of the poets represented here see ekphrastic art as representing a literal description of an art work (for example Nathan Langston's 'translation of images into words';) other poets see it as an interpretation of what is behind or beyond the scenes/brushstrokes (Hedy Habra's 'offering an imagined version of what might have happened before or after the portrayed scene'). Jane Burn is explicit that 'ekphrasis for me goes well beyond description of the artwork itself', and Bob Beagrie talks of 'scrying' in a typically mystical approach to how visions can offer insight. In their different ways, each poet at least glances at the Greek etymology of the term – the calling or speaking out, by 'naming' an inanimate object (nicely explained by Dominique Hecq). The 'sources' for the ekphrastic responses are diverse, and include ballet productions (Amina Alyal and Jen Webb); music and music videos (Toby Fitch, Paul Munden, Jessica Wilkinson); and the more expected art works.

Perhaps perversely I have not in this review quoted from any of the poems themselves; with this book more than many I have read, it seemed almost invidious to do so. In these pages there is such a richness of individual insight, expressing a continuing evolving collective experience, that for just one reader to select certain lines would be an injustice to the whole. Ekphrasis is, by its very nature, a relational activity; with that in mind this seems a good place to mention the ongoing Telephone project (https://phonebook.gallery) being conducted by Nathan Langston, which brings poets from all over the world into dialogue with each other through responding to randomly allocated images. Buy the book; read it; share it. Write your own responses.

It took me a long time to read the book – in fact I am still dipping into it and finding new delights and puzzles – it was reassuring to learn that one poem took ten years to write (Lorette C Luzajic). Perhaps this stands as a testimony to the importance of this art form and to the whole process of creativity itself, such a precious and irreplaceable activity/artefact in this world of cynical functionality and commodification in which the bean counters and broligarchy are so determined to erode any engagement with or investment in the arts, humanities, and all that supports the business of being human.

Hannah Stone

Diverted to Split by Hugh McMillan
Luath Press Ltd
ISBN: 978-1-80425-140-9 pp115 £9.99

.... 'Why, in a world
of unfettered misery, this is a Dry Train
is never explained. It is bad enough
travelling to England in the first place.' ('Dry Train')

This summer I went to "The Wee Gaitherin", a wonderful three-day poetry festival in Stonehaven, near Aberdeen, where I heard some fine poetry, often from writers I had never heard of: Hugh McMillan was one of these new-to-me poets. Judging by the reception he got as he took the stage – and later seeing the number of publications he has under his belt – the fault is entirely mine.

Diverted to Split is the work of a poet of considerable talents, combining a keen eye for the arresting details of everyday life, a laconic turn of phrase, humour ('Makars'), and no small love for the people and the world around him. The collection bursts with memorable characters, like the eponymous 'Bitter Old Men' on the 'shell of a bus rattling towards Stranraer,' who spend five verses complaining about the youth of today, before two girls get on and the men, who were not expecting youth, 'recoil as if before radiation'. Or the barman who had just purchased a huge crossbow and wanted to fire it 'to see what happened'. While in 'Kirkcudbright Graffiti' we are invited to consider the eponymous tragedy of 'Dougie No Cock', among others.

McMillan has an enviable flair for titles: 'Appreciating Botticelli's Birth of Venus after a Bad Piece of Fish'; 'Keats in the Maxwell Arms', 'Dalbeattie (Most folk thought he was a thief or an army spy: such is the lot of poets)'; 'Just Another Bog-Standard Sea Poem,' from which,

> 'Earlier he said
> he is not allowed beer because
> it makes him into a sadist
> and I told him I am not allowed
> beer because of the rash on my leg.'

Plus, my own favourite, 'Today's Funeral' which:

> 'scored 4 on the funeral scale
> point off for him being younger
> than me.'

It is a collection full of humour, joy and love, all wrapped in warm humanity. My overwhelming feeling coming away from reading it is that McMillan is a person with whom I could enjoy taking a bus journey through a gloomy, rain-soaked Galloway and share a few drinks, while chewing over the business of the day: as he write in 'Mythos'

> 'In such weather
> dreaming is simply
> borrowing from tomorrow.'

Nick Allen

Strange Husbandry by Lorcán Black
Seren
ISBN: 9781781727447   £10.99

This is the second collection by the Irish-born poet, Lorcán Black. He is well-published in journals and has several prestigious prize nominations to boot. It is not hard to see why, as this collection is fast-paced, emotionally powerful, diverse in inspiration and full of characters – some historical and some not. Many poems emerge from Black's long association with London:

> 'London settles itself
> within me' ('The Anthology of Trees')

but it is never home – also it is a London beset by Covid, the Russian invasion of Ukraine and riven with queer passion and complex relationships. It is an intense ride as Black pulls no punches and is willing to get to grips with some disturbing subject matter. Allen Ginsberg once described poetry as 'that time of night, lying in bed, thinking what you really think, making the private world public, that's what the poet does.' That certainly is what Black does and with fearlessness, high technical ability and a facility for the killing phrase that brooks no disagreement.

Covid happened some years ago now but Black's poems perfectly bring back the horror:

'Look/how quiet it is here –
how tight the night bites you' ('Lockdown") –

but with almost a sideways look which renders the poems less period pieces and more a lament for the essential sadness. 'Hazmat' turns paramedics collecting an infected person into beekeepers,

'carefully arranging
the contagious fever of a whole hot hive
to be hand-delivered
into a white sterility.'

Black has a facility for allowing the ordinary object to carry, explain and offload the heavy weight of remembering. In a poem dedicated to a dead friend, the narrator walks through her Dublin accommodation where everything seen and touched has the potential for pain.

'I remember: a teacup abandoned,
milk curdling deep

in the swell of its belly'

and how

' …when I tried to,
my shook, white hand failed
utterly to move it'. ('26 Charleville Mall').

It is the technique of the best news photographers, where a single displaced object is freighted with overwhelming emotional heft of the wider picture. A similar motif is used in Black's engagement with the Russian invasion of Ukraine. 'Bucha', which deals with the massacre early in the war of several hundred Ukrainian civilians, starts,

'You have to remember, at some point
someone was taking butter out of a butter dish
when the windows blew in.'

Such delicacy reminds us powerfully that the victims are not 'victims' but humans like us and to ground/contrast the absurd horror in/with mundane lived experiences.

Many poems focus on historical/mythical characters which, apart from demonstrating that poetry can be made from many sources also

Dream Catcher 51

demonstrates a certain view of the continuity of violent inhumanity. Giles Corey is pressed to death in Salem because he won't plead when accused of witchcraft (thus saving his estate but not his life). Black's focus is often on women – 'Hyaptia', a stunning study of the torture and murder of the fifth century philosopher by a gang of radical Christian monks; Salome; the mythical Circe and Juno all appear as strong and, in their ways, empowered women – and, maybe, offer a counter narrative to toxic masculinity.

Black can see and take on the world as cruel and damaged/damaging but he never loses sight of compassion, care and, indeed, family – here are beautiful poems about his mother and sister, the former imagined as Louise to his Thelma. There are also many poems about sex, love and relationships, endings and beginnings. The title poem is a powerful study of sexual jealousy – a lover keeps the phone number of a previous partner on his phone, who

> 'swims up from the depths every darkness – like some gaping, terrible fish'

– and ways out of such an abyss. A ghost wanders about his ex-partner's house, jealous:

> 'I cry for the glance
> you probably give him
> on a Saturday morning naked, in bed,
> in pure shone light...'('An Bhean Se/The Banshee'

which, interestingly, can be read with the revenant as male or, given the literal meaning of the Irish, as a woman.)

This is a marvellous collection which rewards close attention. If you read nothing else the poignant and glorious sequence, 'The Descent from the Cross', based on a painting from the studio of Rembrandt, and which plays with the possibility of an erotic ('I feel the softness of his curls still'), charged relationship between Mary Magdalene and the man brought down, crucified, from the cross. It is lyrical, handled by Black as if it, itself, was the love object and shows Black's craft and the deep emotional life from which these poems emerge.

Patrick Lodge

New and Selected Poems by Paul Sutherland
Valley Press
ISBN: 978-1-908853-77-6 pp380 £20

Sutherland's meaty collection is broken into multiple sections, reflecting different stages of his many decades as a wordsmith and sojourner, and capturing his personal and spiritual progressions. Many of them are autobiographical in nature, disclosing a pattern of migration and belonging, a sense of being tethered to family roots whilst also feeling rootless and restless: he describes experiencing himself as an 'intimate-alien', when flying back to the UK (where he has lived for over fifty years) from a visit to family in Canada. This unsettledness acts as grit in the oyster, forming the basis of many of his poems. The complex threads of personal and communal history in his native land surface clearly in some of these poems, though he also honours his current home in Lincolnshire, and records visits to Cyprus, York, Oxford, the United States, Scotland and more.

Although billed as *New and Selected Poems*, there are significant chunks of prose in some of the selections, for example in 'Spires and Minarets' (which captures 'impressions in poems and prose' of walking through the Lincolnshire fens); 'Long Sutton Day' and 'Finding a Blue Door in Oxford' also feature journal-style entries, punctuated by short poems which resemble haiku:

> fresh green seduces
> someone endeared turns their back
> on the world again.

The economy of terse three line stanzas clearly appeals to him, although elsewhere we find passages with more extended lyricism, such as the evocative lines from 'No Trains in Cyprus';

> '...on the fens,
> so primed for flight, assembled swans
>   all at once hesitate. Afternoon passes.'

Sutherland's spiritual transition into a Sufi Muslim permeates his later work, though extracts from a sequence of poems on Holy Week demonstrate that his spirituality reaches beyond this to an appreciation for Christian mysticism. Sometimes we are given notes to provide context or further information, such as the glossary of Scottish terms at the end of the two Scotland and the Isles poems; however this assistance is not offered for the poems about Sutherland's Sufi beliefs. A more consistent approach to providing notes would really support the reader in fully appreciating these poems (I tried and failed to find out about Naheebahweequay, though I presume I got close with the variant spelling Nahnebahwequay?). I imagine this inconsistency in approach is due to the 'collected' nature of work from many different sources, some of which may have adopted a different approach to endnotes.

As Ian Duhig notes in his endorsement 'epic and intimate scales overlap'; in the massive output represented here are forays into erotic encounters; tender moments of farewell ('Washing your Corpse' is a stand out piece); questions to be answered about how time and memory are experienced; juxtaposed to these 'big' issues are apparently trivial conversations with fellow travellers, the contents of shelves in grocery stores and other quotidian minutiae. Such a weighty tome demands repeat visits to mine all its treasures.

Hannah Stone

Exit Strategy by Patrick White
Broken Sleep Books
ISBN: 978-1-9-1693871-7 £9.99

>'I offer no trigger warning, no disclaimer.
>I'm coming at you with a switchblade.'
>('Postcard: untitled. (before Mark Rothko))

Some poetry is written to the heart, some to the guts and some to the intellect: Patrick White's rigorous exploration of grief, beauty, loss, in particular the loss of a great love, falls unapologetically into the latter category.

The superb 'Limnal Worlds' opens the collection and aptly enough sets the tone with the refrains,

>'between morphine & biopsy...
>between syringe & stitch...
>between a single cell & metastasis.'

while 'torn apart by change' from 'Metanoia' provides the overview.

>'You clawed at sheets, tried to eat inedible
>Things' ('Shroud');

>'I am the wound & the blade' ('Exist Strategy')

>'I am the broken television
>unable to receive a signal' ('Cold Room')

The collection captures White standing astride loss, its abyss all around and unavoidable, except the poet is not wishing to avoid, but rather to stare deeper into, in an attempt to understand or at least fathom where grief ends. Because of this, I am most drawn to Rothko as the artistic touchstone for the collection, although I also see fine connectivity with the works of Anselm Kiefer and Francesca Woodman (both referenced).

>'What's hard is living, once touched by fire' ('Negative Space')

>'Darkness I've come to realise is a privilege –
>known at 4am & sleepless
>the sun rising like a scalpel' ('Cold Dark Matter').

A good half of the poems are noted as being "after…" someone, (while others are "before" and "alongside" – which I don't understand), usually referencing an artist, many of which were not known to me; the book is consciously ekphrastic. It is a challenging, confronting collection. This is not said to diminish the work, which is estimable, but to note where the bar is set.

I broke the habit of a lifetime and looked up every reference and word I didn't know … and the collection blossomed, became three-dimensional: the question remains, should that be necessary?

Nick Allen

Kindling by Julie Burke
Five Leaves New Poetry
ISBN: 9781915434197, £7.00, pp 44
and

Miniskirts in the Waste Land by Pralibha Castle
The Hedgehog Poetry Press, 34 pages
ISBN: 978193499747, pp 34.

Though different in style, mood and theme, these two poetry pamphlets show the importance of small independent presses in giving good but little-known poets a voice. Both collections ought to be more readily available. They show the diversity and quality of contemporary British poetry.

Kindling is perhaps the most accessible. It draws heavily on the poet's memory and observation, often light heartedly playing with images and form. I was captivated by the opening lines of the first poem, 'Music therapy':

'When I first met my aunt's piano
music found my fingers
and emerged, stomping…'

Burke's poems often give us snapshots of people and scenes that have featured in her life. There is a strong sense of place, especially of the coast. Some of the poems are gently humorous, like 'Soulmates' and 'New Learner', or 'Conchology'; others express deep emotion. 'Buds', for example, conveys the strength of a friendship that began in 1973 on the first day at a new school.

'I love you – my spirit's sister, my Best Bud.

'I'll never tell you that.
You'd just tell me to 'shuddup'
and call me a prat…'

Several of the poems deal with the loss of loved ones, portrayed through images and objects rather than by direct expressions of emotion. 'Mysteries of the rosary' is a moving portrayal of dementia:

> 'Clobbered again by the things he's forgotten,
> not just the everyday *Where's my stick?* Or *What day is it?*
> forgotten,
> but solid gone forgotten…'

The ending is deeply sad, yet hopeful. Though the loved one has forgotten how 'to make/the sign of the cross,' he still connects

> 'in a tow rope through time,
> all the way to the heaven
> he still remembers.'

Technically, *Kindling* is quietly successful too. The form of each poem varies but fits the mood and tone. There are amusing concrete poems like 'Kite', 'Finding Athena', 'The Dinner Party' and 'Displacement activities'. Sometimes the viewpoint is unusual, as in 'Do urban gulls dream of the distant ocean?' and 'Workhorses'. It is the deeply personal poems that stay with me, however. 'In between days' captures the stage of grief between immediate loss and being able to think fondly of the lost one, while 'Mum's rules for a long and happy life' captures a whole generation of women now gone.

The atmosphere and style of *Miniskirts in The Waste Land* is very different, recalling the vibrancy of the '60's and early '70's. There is a strong sense of period and place throughout. The cover design and title catch the reader's attention, and the first poem (also the title poem) sets the tone. Seen through the eyes of a Convent schoolgirl, it captures what it was like to be young then, and establishes the period by unobtrusive references to its music and films. The link with TS Eliot's *The Waste Land* comes through the girl's studies:

> 'That term they read *The Waste Land*. Eliot's
> words get her in the gut *them pills I took*
> *to bring it off.* Opaque as trig, sixth form
> sniggers outside tit and second base eavesdropped
> in the locker rooms between hockey and maths…'

The seedy glamour of London is caught in poems that depict the colourful market areas, with 'gutters a carnage/of jaundiced cabbages, mossy lemons/a tulip, crushed.' ('Reflections'). Sharply observed details convey the loneliness of bed-sitter land in 'Lizzie's Trip Down Portobello':

> 'Corner of All Saints and Portobello,
> women huddle. Hens
> flocking. Pecking gossip.
> Princess Margaret scarves
> knotted tight as knuckles …'

Castle's poems are never merely descriptive, however. They can suddenly shock, like 'Octopus Ride', where a fairground attraction turns into fear of miscarrying a child. There are moments of happiness and love, as in 'My Saviour', but even there, the easy-going landlady's conversation is recalled as 'gossip hawked up/on a phlegmy Belfast cackle'. Language and imagery often fizz with originality, as in 'an anarchy of hankies' ('In the Attic') or 'noses cat-close' ('Artichokes').

There are gentler poems like 'Leaven' and 'The Quickening,' both of which are touching portrayals of motherhood. 'When I read About The War' recalls Vietnam and those who went missing. The last two stanzas are beautifully restrained, as the speaker recalls the day the airmail arrived 'like a moth/blue as your eyes...' and she read:

'Jeff mentioned you
The dude dropped by
Jeff's missing
Jeff's sister Jane'

The sense of betrayal grows throughout the collection, as the setting moves to the India many escaped to in the '60's, looking for spiritual fulfilment, only to find poverty and disappointment. The imagery becomes more vivid and the appeal to the senses stronger. The sequence of poems beginning with 'Seeking *Moksha*' conveys the exotic squalor of life in a hot country, on the edge of society. That poem has stayed with me, with its depiction of Radha, 'Known back in Hove as Sue', finding cockroaches in her fridge and being terrified by a rat, then comforted by 'Krishna in a saggy nappy'. 'Down Mahatma Gandhi Road' depicts abject poverty without sentimentality:

'Baksheesh, baba, paese pae.
Heads jiggle. Gruel-shrill wails.
Wrists a bangle-clash of need.'

The final poem 'To the Beach' offers some resolution. Its image of saving a butterfly from a spider's web reminds us of the beauty of nature:

'Blue wings
graze her skin,
an electric memory
of eyelashes
against her cheek...'

I can recommend both collections. I wonder whether memory and close observation will provide as much material for future poets, now that we are looking down at screens, rather than around us?

Pauline Kirk

INDEX OF AUTHORS

Adam Strickson 31, 88, 115
Andrew Pearson 104, 106
Andrew Senior 77
Andria Jane Cooke 91
Angela Brodie 70, 122, 146
Ann Preston 52, 55
Annie Kocur 64, 107
Barbara Howerska 20, 137
Carolyn Oulton 24
Cathryn M. Spiller 87
Charles Lomas 61, 85, 116
Christopher Webster 66
Claire Booker 94, 152, 158
Clare Bryden 79
Clare Starling ... 23, 96, 125, 160
Clifford Liles 65
Connie Greig 62
Cosmo Goldsmith 56
Craig Martin Getz 32
D G Herring 35
Dave Foxton 136
Dave Wynne-Jones 63, 163
David Olsen 49, 117
David Sapp 92
Denise Bennett 30
Elaine Ewart 82, 83, 134
Greg Forshaw 110
Greg McGee 1
Hannah Stone 3, 165, 169
Heather Deckner 98, 120
Helen Scadding 59
Ian Chapman 153
Jack Granath 58
Jane Newberry 21, 114
Jean Atkin 29
Jennifer Harrison 138

Jet McDonald 81, 129
John Scarborough 95, 121
Kat Couch 38
Keith Willson 127, 159
Kristina Diprose 37
Laura Reanna Smith 22, 25
Lauren K. Nixon 50, 89
Lisa Falshaw 74, 101
Louise Worthington 75
Marius Grose 102, 128
Mark Pearce 67
Martin Reed 69, 105
Nick Allen 166, 171
Nick Cooke 161
Pamela Coren 72, 119, 133
Patrick Lodge 167
Paul Bavister 57, 97
Paul Brownsey 140
Pauline Kirk 172
Phil Knight 27
Phil Vernon 48
Rachel Goodman 90
Ralph Dartford 12, 14, 15
Ray Malone 109
Richard Smith 99, 124
Rosie Jackson 41, 76
Sarah J Bryson 47, 126
Shaun Barr 19, 40, 103
Simon French 78, 131, 164
Simon Tindale 118
Stuart Handysides 46
Sue Spiers 151
Tom Ratcliffe 16, 18, 60, 132
Tom Vaughan 51, 86
Wilf Deckner 33, 34

Other anthologies and collections available from Stairwell Books

Village Fox	Richard Cave
An Anxiety of Poets in their Natural Habitat	Amina Alyal
First of All I Wrote Your Name	Winston Plowes
Sleeve Heart	Eleanor May Blackburn
Goldfish	Jonathan Aylett
Strike	Sarah Wimbush
Marginalia	Doreen Hinchliffe
The Estuary and the Sea	Jennifer Keevill
In | Between	Angela Arnold
Quiet Flows the Hull	Clint Wastling
Lunch on a Green Ledge	Stella Davis
there is an england	Harry Gallagher
Iconic Tattoo	Richard Harries
Herdsmenization	Ngozi Olivia Osuoha
On the Other Side of the Beach, Light	Daniel Skyle
Words from a Distance	Ed. Amina Alyal, Judi Sissons
Fractured	Shannon O'Neill
Unknown	Anna Rose James, Elizabeth Chadwick Pywell
When We Wake We Think We're Whalers from Eden	Bob Beagrie
Awakening	Richard Harries
Starspin	Graehame Barrasford Young
A Stray Dog, Following	Greg Quiery
Blue Saxophone	Rosemary Palmeira
Steel Tipped Snowflakes 1	Izzy Rhiannon Jones, Becca Miles, Laura Voivodeship
Where the Hares Are	John Gilham
The Glass King	Gary Allen
Gooseberries	Val Horner
Poetry for the Newly Single 40 Something	Maria Stephenson
Northern Lights	Harry Gallagher
More Exhibitionism	Ed. Glen Taylor
The Beggars of York	Don Walls
Lodestone	Hannah Stone
Learning to Breathe	John Gilham
Throwing Mother in the Skip	William Thirsk-Gaskill
New Crops from Old Fields	Ed. Oz Hardwick
The Ordinariness of Parrots	Amina Alyal
Homeless	Ed. Ross Raisin
Somewhere Else	Don Walls
Taking the Long Way Home	Steve Nash
Pressed by Unseen Feet	Ed. Rose Drew, Alan Gillott

For further information please contact rose@stairwellbooks.com
www.stairwellbooks.co.uk

@stairwellbooks

www.ingramcontent.com/pod-product-compliance
Ingram Content Group UK Ltd.
Pitfield, Milton Keynes, MK11 3LW, UK
UKHW020116210825
462076UK00001B/1